THE ANAESTHETICS OF ARCHITECTURE

THE ANAESTHETICS OF ARCHITECTURE

NEIL LEACH

The MIT Press
Cambridge, Massachusetts
London, England

Second printing, 2000

Every effort has been made to trace the original copyright holders of the images reproduced in this book, and to obtain permission to reproduce them.

This book was set in Garamond 3 and Meta and was printed and bound in the United States of America.

Library of Congress Cataloging-in-Publication Data

Leach, Neil.
    The anaesthetics of architecture / Neil Leach.
        p.   cm.
    Includes bibliographical references and index.
    ISBN 0-262-62126-6 (pbk. : alk. paper)
        1. Architecture—Philosophy.   I. Title.
NA2500.L43   1999
720'.1—DC21

98-37597
CIP

CONTENTS

PREFACE   vii

ACKNOWLEDGMENTS   ix

1   SATURATION OF THE IMAGE   1

2   THE ARCHITECT AS FASCIST   17

3   THE AESTHETICS OF INTOXICATION   33

4   THE ARCHITECTURE OF THE CATWALK   55

5   SEDUCTION, THE LAST RESORT   71

NOTES   89

INDEX   99

PREFACE

This is a polemical work. In an age when manifestos and polemics have become somewhat unfashionable, such a work may appear out of place. Yet it is precisely because Western culture has developed into a largely tolerant, pluralistic society, dominated by a mild-mannered political correctness, that this book is so necessary. In an architectural culture whose liberal openness is always prone to collapse into a libertarian conformity, it will have a particular relevance. The book will no doubt prove controversial, but if it succeeds only in eliciting criticism, it will have achieved its primary objective of stirring up debate in what is perceived as an all too complacent domain.

The text is often extreme in its argumentation. In this it follows the "fatal strategies" of Jean Baudrillard of pushing analyses to their limit. If, therefore, many of the arguments appear to be somewhat exaggerated, and to lead on occasions to potentially absurd generalizations, these should be recognized as part of a deliberate strategy. The text offers less a representation of reality than a transfiguration of it, while nonetheless aiming to highlight a real problem within contemporary architectural culture.

The book draws on contemporary philosophy and cultural theory. In particular, it seeks to offer an overview of a tradition of critical European thinking on the subject of the image, beginning with the work of Walter Benjamin and others, and continuing through to Guy

Debord and Baudrillard. While these thinkers do not share an identical outlook—indeed there are many differences and tensions between their respective positions—taken as a whole, their work offers a powerful critique of the role of the image. By bringing this critique to bear on the domain of architecture, the book seeks to open the discipline to fresh ideas and challenge the often unrigorous thinking that has dominated it in recent years.

The premise behind the book is that architects have become increasingly obsessed with images and image-making, to the detriment of their discipline. The sensory stimulation induced by these images may have a narcotic effect that diminishes social and political awareness, leaving architects cosseted within their aesthetic cocoons, remote from the actual concerns of everyday life. In the intoxicating world of the image, it is argued, the aesthetics of architecture threaten to become the *anaesthetics* of architecture. The intoxication of the aesthetic leads to an aesthetics of intoxication, and a consequent lowering of critical awareness. What results is a culture of mindless consumption, where there is no longer any possibility of meaningful discourse. In such a culture the only effective strategy is one of seduction. Architectural design is reduced to the superficial play of empty, seductive forms, and philosophy is appropriated as an intellectual veneer to justify these forms.

ACKNOWLEDGMENTS

The origins of this book lie in discussions held within the Critical Theory group at the University of Nottingham. I am indebted to the students in the MA program in Architecture and Critical Theory at Nottingham and to my colleagues who have taught on this course for their contributions to these discussions.

I am grateful to colleagues and friends for their support over the years, especially to those who have lent me advice on this particular book. These include Andrew Benjamin, Peter Carl, Sarah Chaplin, Matt Connell, Darren Deane, David Frisby, Graeme Gilloch, Jonathan Hale, Vaughan Hart, Paul Hegarty, Eric Holding, Bill Hutson, Eleonore Kofman, Susan Marks, Bernard McGuirk, Jo Moss, Giles Peaker, Doina Petrescu, Jane Rendell, Katrina Ruedi, Joseph Rykwert, Ioana Sandi, Yvonne Sherratt, Jon Simons, Christina Ujma, Dalibor Vesely, Sarah Wigglesworth, Rosemary Wilson, and Tracey Winton.

Finally, I would like to thank Roger Conover for his unswerving enthusiasm for this project from the very outset.

THE ANAESTHETICS OF ARCHITECTURE

1

SATURATION OF THE IMAGE

Our present condition has been described in terms of an "ecstasy of communication."[1] In the media society of today, technological advances in telecommunications and in methods of visual reproduction ensure that we are constantly being inundated with images. Televisions, faxes, photocopiers, and computers have become the virtual windows of the age of the information highway, conduits of digitalized impulses that link the individual with a global network of communications. The modern office and home are deluged with reproduced images and information: news on the hour, every hour; movies previewed, premiered, released, cloned into videos, and drip-fed through cable TV. It is a culture of the copy, a society of saturation, the second flood. The world has become "xeroxized" to infinity.[2]

It has generally been assumed that this inundation of images leads to an "information society" which promotes a high level of communication. Yet according to some commentators, this "ecstasy of communication" has precisely the opposite effect: "We live in a world," as the French cultural theorist Jean Baudrillard has postulated, "where there is more and more information, and less and less meaning."[3] It is precisely in this infinite cloning of the image, in this infinite proliferation of signs, that the sign itself has become invisible. The sign no longer has any meaning. This leads him to question what prompts this situation. Is it that information "produces" meaning but the process is "leaky," so that the system founders like a ship? According to this thesis, "despite efforts to reinject meaning and content, meaning is lost and devoured faster than it can be rejected."[4] Or is it that information has nothing to do with signification, in that information is a purely technical medium, to which meaning is then attached? Or is it finally, as Baudrillard suggests, that there is a negative link between the two, and that information either destroys or neutralizes meaning? In this case "the loss of meaning is directly linked to the dissolving, dissuasive action of information, the media, and the mass media."[5]

It is this final model that Baudrillard pursues, one that challenges the commonly held assumption that information generates meaning:

Everywhere information is thought to produce an accelerated circulation of meaning, a plus value of meaning homologous to the economic one that results from the accelerated rotation of capital. Information is thought to create communication, and even if the waste is enormous, a general consensus would have it that nevertheless, as a whole, there be an excess of meaning.

For Baudrillard, then, while we think that information generates meaning, in fact the opposite occurs. It is precisely the surfeit of information that denies meaning: "Information devours its own content. It devours communication and the social." Baudrillard ascribes this seemingly paradoxical situation to two factors. First, information, rather than creating communication, "exhausts itself in the process of communication." Thus meaning is itself also exhausted in the staging of meaning. Second, according to Baudrillard, the pressure of information "pursues an irresistible destructuration of the social." "Thus information dissolves meaning and dissolves the social, in a sort of nebulous state dedicated not to a surplus of innovation, but, on the contrary, to total entropy."[6] Baudrillard gives the example of a twelve-volume report by the Exxon Corporation, a report so vast that no one could possibly absorb its information: "Exxon: the American government requests a complete report on the multinational's activities throughout the world. The result is twelve 1,000 page volumes, whose reading alone, not to mention the analysis, would exceed a few years work. Where is the information?"[7] This situation is exacerbated by our cultural situation, dominated as it is, in Baudrillard's terms, by simulation and hyperreality. The image itself has become the new reality, or hyper-reality—a virtual world floating above the real world in its own sealed-off hermetic envelope. It is a world that has lost touch with its referents in the real world, and where, paradoxically, the term "real" has been hijacked by the multinational conglomerates and turned into an empty advertising slogan, claiming its authenticity against its very absence of authenticity, such that "authenticity" becomes a suspect, counterfeit currency in the hypermarket of hyperreality. It's the "real thing," a Coca-Cola world of industrially manufactured "natural" ingredients, a dream world of commodities seemingly conjured up from nowhere and paid for with computerized, invisible credit.

In a world where the imaginary becomes the "real," there is no longer a place for the real. In the "perfect crime" of the twentieth century, reality itself has been stolen.[8] Nowhere has the cover-up been more obvious than in Disneyland, the archetypal dream-center of this culture of consumption. For Disneyland, as Baudrillard notes, presents itself as an imaginary world, a make-believe kingdom to be contrasted with the real world outside. And its greatest success is to make us believe that it is make-believe. Disneyland thereby lends authority to the world outside; it is an imaginary world that becomes a "prop" to the real, a make-believe kingdom that makes us believe that the world outside is real. Yet it is here that the greatest deceit takes place. For the world outside belongs no longer to the "real" but to the hyperreal. And Disneyland, as Baudrillard observes, is precisely part of that hyperreal world outside. It is the very replication of the values of America; and if the population buys into this myth of the make-believe, it is simply because it wants to buy into it. Disneyfication has become the new religion of the twentieth century, where dream and reality are entangled in a never-never world brought to you by Disney Products Plc, purveyors of dreams to the universe.

The corollary also holds true, in that the world outside is equally part of Disney. The whole of Western culture has been consumed by this syndrome. In this context the objections raised against the presence

1.1 Castle, Eurodisney. Photo: Disney.

of a "fake" Eurodisney castle in France, a country whose architectural legacies include the "authentic" châteaux of the Loire, appear somewhat hollow. For the question is not so much whether a castle is "authentic" or not, but whether we can any longer claim the capacity to grasp its authenticity. In a culture where capitalism absorbs our heritage into the framework of commodified tourist "experiences," the line between authenticity and inauthenticity becomes somewhat blurred. In the age of hyperreality, the Eiffel Tower is appropriated as the "Eiffel Tower Experience" and Notre-Dame as the "Notre-Dame Experience." And when the authentic engagement with the inauthentic collapses into the inauthentic engagement with the authentic, how can we guarantee that we will ever access the historical "reality" of France? It is in the figure of Eurodisney, then, that we glimpse the essential nature of tourism today. Eurodisney, Eiffel Tower, Notre-Dame, châteaux on the Loire. Roll up, roll up for the hyperreal coach tour of the universe.

The Aestheticization of the World

On the slippery slope into a culture of simulation, the function of the image shifts from reflecting reality to masking and perverting that reality. Once reality itself has been removed, all we are left with is a world of images, of hyperreality, of pure simulacra. The detachment of these images from their original complex cultural situation decontextualizes them. They are fetishized and judged by their surface appearance at the expense of any deeper reading. This culture of reification objectifies the whole act of viewing, such that any appreciation of depth, perspective, or relief is reduced, promoting instead "a gaze which sweeps over objects without seeing in them anything other than their objectiveness."[9] In the process of reading an object as a mere image, that object is emptied of much of its original meaning.[10]

The image is all there is. Everything is transported into an aesthetic realm and valued for its appearance. The world has become aestheticized. Everything has become appropriated as art. As Baudrillard himself comments, "Art has today totally penetrated reality. . . . The aestheticization of the world is complete."[11] Baudrillard locates this problem within a series of more general symptoms, the transpolitical, transsexual, and transaesthetic condition of contemporary culture. This is the condition of excess, when everything becomes political, sexual, and aesthetic, and, consequently, any specificity in these domains is lost. For just as when everything takes on a political meaning, politics itself become invisible, and when everything takes on a sexual meaning, sex itself becomes invisible, so too when everything becomes aesthetic, the very notion of art disappears. As a consequence of this, for Baudrillard, the word *aesthetics* loses all meaning: "When everything becomes aesthetic, nothing is either beautiful or ugly any longer, and art itself disappears."[12]

Baudrillard describes this condition of excess as one of "obscenity," which he characterizes as "the endless, unbridled proliferation of the social, of the political, of information, of the economic, of the aesthetic, not to mention, of course, the sexual."[13] Associated with this is the notion of "obesity." Within the "obscenity" of the present, the saturation of the aesthetic has led to a state of "obesity." And it is this absorption of everything into the realm of art, this swelling and distension of the category, that ensures that all it contains is effectively obliterated.

In a culture of simulacra and simulation, a culture of hyperreality where the image has become a new reality, the domain that governs the image—aesthetics—has come to dominate other domains: "Everything aestheticizes itself: politics aestheticizes itself into the spectacle, sex into advertising and pornography, and the whole gamut of activities into what is held to be called culture, which is something totally different from art; this culture is an advertising and media semiologizing process which invades everything."[14] The model here is a paradoxical one. The very liberation of the notion of a work of art has led to the abandonment of any fundamental rules for a work of art. And if there is no standard against which to measure a work of art, there can equally be no standard by which to appreciate it. Instead of aesthetic judgment we find an obscene fascination with excess. There is a paradox, too, in terms of the art market. The escalation in production of works of art leads to a paralysis of the principles that govern them. Hyperacceleration leads to deceleration. Explosion leads to implosion. Frenzy leads to stasis. And so the art market, for Baudrillard, reaches saturation and becomes stifled: "There is a necessary relation between the rupture with all logic of aesthetic value within the field of art, and the rupture with all logic of mercantile value, within the market of art. The same mechanical racing, the same madness, the same excess of simulation characterize them both."[15]

This "racing," this acceleration by inertia, only leads to its opposite, a cultural meltdown, a state of supersaturation where even anti-art objects become appropriated as art; and no domain of the physical world will escape this process: "The whole industrial machinery of the world found itself aestheticized, the whole insignificance of the world found itself transfigured by aesthetics. . . . Everything, even the most insignificant, the most marginal, the most obscene encultures itself, becomes a museum piece, and aestheticizes itself."[16] And this catastrophe folds back on the art world itself, which, for Baudrillard, is forced to dematerialize itself through minimalism and hence erase itself: "Because the world in its entirety is destined to the play of operational aesthetics, art has no other recourse than to disappear."[17]

In sum, the surfeit of the image—the excess of communication and information—implies the opposite, a reduction of communication and information. All this is exacerbated under the condition of hyperreality, whereby content is consumed and absorbed within a general process of aestheticization. The world therefore threatens to be perceived increasingly in terms of a proliferation of aesthetic images empty of content.

The Politics of Aestheticization

The question of how the process of aestheticization robs objects of content seems at first sight somewhat problematic: the popular assumption is that works of art necessarily embody meaning, especially in the case of Marxist art where, as Walter Benjamin has observed, artists are always striving to politicize their work.[18] Yet is the question of quite how art embodies that content so straightforward that anyone not familiar with the *intended* meaning of a work of art would recognize that meaning, even if it were abstract art? For if we exclude slogans and posters that rely heavily on words and more obvious methods of visual signification in order to communicate specific messages, the primary role of art is not to serve as a literal form of communication. Indeed the bare fact remains that there can usually be no single privileged reading to a work of art. Meaning, in this sense, often becomes a question of symbolic meaning. It is limited to what might be conveyed to a particular individual. And symbolic meaning, as Fredric Jameson has observed, "is as volatile as the arbitrariness of the sign."[19]

It might be useful here to take up Jameson's notion of allegory in the context of political content. To view artistic form as inherently "politicized" is, for Jameson, a misguided project: "It was one of the signal errors of the artistic activism of the 1960s to suppose that there existed, in advance, forms that were in and of themselves endowed with a political, and even revolutionary, potential by virtue of their own intrinsic properties."[20] For Jameson, political content does not reside in artistic form. It is merely projected onto it by a process that is strictly allegorical. To perceive the political meaning, one has to understand the allegorical system in which it is encoded.[21] In the collective imagination, of course, this process of projection on the part of the interpreting agent is somehow overlooked. The very "ventriloquism" of ascribing a meaning to a work of art is never fully acknowledged, so that in the hermeneutic moment that meaning appears to be a property of the work itself.

Jameson stresses the ephemerality of that projection of political content onto form: any political content may subsequently be erased or rewritten.[22] Political content is a question of allegorical content, which depends upon the retention of memory of some narrative explanation of what an artwork is *supposed* to mean. But this does not undermine the fact that in a given place, at a given time, and for a given group of people, a work of art will inevitably be seen as the concrete embodiment of certain political values. Indeed, while for Jameson form in itself is

"inert," it must be recognized that the artwork is never decontextualized. Art will therefore always have a "meaning," but this meaning is
merely projected onto it and is determined by factors such as context,
use, and associations.[23]

What is crucial is the "social ground" of an artwork. When
removed from its contextual situation, pure artistic form would be
exposed for what it is. Form, as Jameson notes, "would lack all political and allegorical efficacy" once taken out of the social and cultural
movements that lend it this force. This is not to deny that art may
indeed have "political and allegorical efficacy," but rather to recognize
that it merely serves as a vehicle for this within a given "social ground."
Once a work becomes abstracted from its original context, once it is
treated in another manner, it changes its meaning. For to decontextu-
alize a work is effectively to desemanticize it, and, by extension, to
recontextualize it is to invest it with another meaning. Moreover, just
as a work of art itself might lose its intended meaning when taken out
of context, so too an object will likewise take on a different meaning
when it becomes treated as a work of art.

Aestheticization therefore leads to a form of depoliticization. This
is not to deny the possibility of politicized art, nor to overlook the
important secondary role of art as a mechanism for consciousness-raising.
Rather it is to acknowledge that the very principle of aestheticization acts
as a constant constraint against the process of politicization. To this
extent, any attempt to politicize art must in essence be compromised.

The Aestheticization of Architecture

While aestheticization remains a background cultural condition that
permeates—to a greater or lesser extent—the whole of present society,
its effects will be all the more marked within a discipline that operates
through the medium of the image. Architecture is fully ensnared within
this condition. For architects engage in a process of aestheticization as
a necessary consequence of their profession. Convention dictates that
architects should see the world in terms of visual representation—

plans, sections, elevations, perspectives, and so on. The world of the architect is a world of the image.

The consequences of this are profound. This privileging of the image has led to an impoverished understanding of the built environment, turning social space into a fetishized abstraction. The space of lived experience has been reduced to a codified system of signification, and with the increasing emphasis on visual perception there has been a corresponding reduction in other forms of sensory perception. "The image kills," as Henri Lefebvre observes, and cannot account for the richness of lived experience.

This condition is further exacerbated by the techniques and systems of representation employed within the architect's office. In a professional culture of parallel motions, set squares, tracing paper, and, ultimately, computers, a culture trapped within the ideological strictures and value-laden hierarchies of capitalism, the separation between spatial practices and representations of space has become complete. The very processes of architectural representation, as Lefebvre observes, have contributed to the aestheticization of design itself, a process serving to obscure many of the underlying constraints that govern architectural practice:

As for the eye of the architect, it is no more innocent than the lot he is given to build on or the blank sheet of paper on which he makes his first sketch. His "subjective" space is freighted with all-too-objective meanings. It is a visual space, a space reduced to blueprints, to mere images—to that "world of the image" which is the enemy of the imagination.[24]

As a consequence, then, of techniques and practices within the office, architects grow increasingly distanced from the world of lived experience. The very fetishizing of the image in architectural culture decontextualizes that image and traps the discourse of architecture within the whole logic of aestheticization, wherein everything is divested of much of its original meaning. Architectural culture, therefore, encounters the same depoliticizing urge that affects all discourses which work within the medium of the aesthetic.

It is precisely when architects claim that their work is *un*aesthetic, when they claim that is it governed by utilitarian concerns in which "art" plays no role, that the risk of aestheticization is most acute. The discourse of functionalism provides an obvious example. For when an architectural element so patently *un*functional as a flat roof belongs to a repertoire of features that come under the definition of "functionalism," the very functionality of functionalism should be treated with some caution. In his incisive critique of the writings of Adolf Loos, the German aesthetic theorist Theodor Adorno has observed that functionalism is little more than an aesthetic category, a form of style. While Loos supported the Kantian distinction between the purpose-free and the purposeful in arguing for a purposeful—or "functional"—architecture, which resists the empty blandishments of purpose-free ornamentation, Adorno notes that the two terms are dialectically related. Supposedly purpose-free arts often have a social function, while there can be no "chemically pure" purposefulness. Even "functional" elements must contain an element of the decorative and cannot remain free of style. "Hence our bitter suspicion is formulated," he concludes: "the absolute rejection of style becomes style."[25]

Furthermore the tendency to privilege the image potentially serves to distance architects from users of their buildings, in that it encourages them to adopt a highly aestheticized outlook, remote from the concerns of the users. This in itself might begin to explain the failure of many modernist architects whose "socially aware" designs were never accepted by the public for whom they were intended. Utopian architectural visions came to be seen as abstract aesthetic experiments of an architectural elite out of touch not only with the taste but also, more importantly, with the practical needs of the populace.

It is most especially in the discourse that surrounds movements such as Brutalism that the contrast between the views of a profession forever gazing through aestheticizing lenses and those of the public is made most obvious. For when such a movement can be turned into an aesthetic landscape by the precious language of architectural commentators, the "reality" of Brutalism, its harsh, uncompromising nature, is overlooked. What to the public appears as a grossly insensitive living environment may be re-presented as a highly sensitive piece of architecture.

1.2 Alison and Peter Smithson, Hunstanton Secondary Modern School, Norfolk, England. Photo: Neil Leach.

It is ironic that Alison and Peter Smithson, the very commentators on Brutalism who purport to celebrate an architecture "without rhetoric," themselves resort to a language markedly rhetorical in its embellishments in order to describe their projects. In this they are caught within their own aesthetic outlook. It is only by adopting a heavily aestheticized language of architectural commentary that they can succeed in dressing up their otherwise uncompromisingly severe architecture. And it is this that allows them to make their extraordinary comparison between the Brutalism of their Hunstanton School project and the simple sensitivity of peasant vernacular architecture:

For us, our Hunstanton School—which probably owes as much to Japanese architecture as to Mies—was the first realisation of our New Brutalism. This particular handling of materials, not in the craft sense but in intellectual appraisal, has been ever-present in the Modern Movement, as indeed familiars of the early German architects have been prompt to remind us. What is new about the New Brutalism among Movements is that it finds its closest affinities not in a past architectural style, but in peasant dwelling forms, which have style and are stylish but were never modish: *a poetry without rhetoric.* We see architecture as a direct statement of a way of life and in the past, ordinary prosaic life has been most succinctly, economically, tersely expressed in the peasant farms and the impedimenta of Mediterranean rural life that Le Corbusier had made respectable.[26]

Commentary on Brutalism is, of course, replete with such comparisons. The Smithsons go on to compare the repetition of their harsh Robin Hood Gardens project in London with the Royal Crescent in Bath and Bernini's colonnade before St. Peter's in Rome.[27] Meanwhile Denys Lasdun speaks of his National Theatre in terms of the ancient theater at Epidaurus in Greece.[28] These comparisons come across as deeply paradoxical. How is it possible for the insensitivity of Brutalism to be compared to the obvious sensitivity of these exquisite works from the past? But the real paradox is that the apparent insensitivity of Brutalism is a direct result of an oversensitivity on the part of the architects. The Smithsons, for example, could hardly be accused of being insensitive about materials, but it is precisely through raising their aesthetic awareness of materials and materiality that the problem has

1.3 Damien Hirst, *The Physical Impossibility of Death in the Mind of Someone Living*, 1991, tiger shark, 5% formaldehyde solution, glass, steel. Photo: Anthony Oliver.

arisen. A heightened receptivity to the coarseness of materials allows those materials to appear sensitive, while to the general public they appear just plain coarse. Aestheticization can therefore be viewed as a way of distorting reality, by privileging aesthetic sensibilities over other background concerns. This may, of course, prove a successful defensive mechanism by providing an aesthetic cocoon from the harsher aspects of that reality. An unpleasant object may be rendered acceptable by adopting such an outlook, so that a disused abattoir might easily be perceived as a potential art gallery. To aestheticize an object is to anaesthetize it and strip it of its unpleasant associations.

The corollary of this is perhaps also true. It may be that the very brutality of Brutalism is what encourages an aesthetic response, just as a disused abattoir might actually present itself as an ideal gallery space. Hence we might reflect upon an artistic culture in which artists such as Damien Hirst have exhibited sharks and other animals dissected and preserved in formaldehyde. The force of these works does not lie solely in their ability to shock the viewer into some form of response. Rather, the very revulsion that they would ordinarily generate, it could be argued, triggers an aestheticized response as a form of defensive mechanism on the part of the viewer, who is already predisposed by the nature of the setting to read these objects as works of art. Consequently, far from compromising their status as serious art, the gruesomeness of these works is precisely what encourages the viewer to treat them as objects worthy of aesthetic contemplation.

In an era of aestheticization, it is those aspects of life that are grim that have the capacity to promote such a seemingly paradoxical response, to the extent that whatever is originally unattractive may easily be deemed aesthetically appealing. In an age when industrialization becomes chic, when former factories are converted into apartments and power stations into national museums, and when industrial footwear and working overalls are treated as fashion items, what is grim and harsh seems to lend itself to aestheticization.

THE ARCHITECT AS FASCIST

Baudrillard's comments on the reduction of meaning within an aestheticized world can be situated within a long tradition of European
thought. Its origins can be traced back if not to Kant himself, then to
the idealism of philosophers after Kant who argued for the autonomy
of the work of art, thereby abstracting it from its social and political
context.[1] This gave rise to the movement of "art for art's sake." But it
was Nietzsche, perhaps, who was the first to articulate comprehensively
the aestheticization of the modern world, in which "truth" was but a
function of the intellect, and "reality" a mere appearance. And in
Nietzsche, too, we find the philosophical foundations of a condition in
which aestheticization realizes its most frightening potential. For it is
with Nietzsche's concept of a "will to power" that the principle of aestheticization might be exploited most cynically. This proved to be the
case when the Nietzschean project was appropriated by the National
Socialists, as a philosophical grounding for the concept of the master
race. And in a world where "truth" is but an illusion, "truth" itself may
be framed and distorted to validate the mythology of history. Once the
process of aestheticization has been harnessed toward the "will to
power," the logical consequence is war and other forms of destruction,
where, as Ansgar Hillach observes, the aestheticization of politics is
fully realized: "What the military and the aestheticist concept of culture have in common in Nietzsche is this: The historically highest and

strictest level of form . . . is called upon to rule as a force over 'barbaric' nature in full affirmation of nihilism in order to generate it to its highest vital power and to bring about the superman. The image of the superman, provisionally seen as a *mythos,* determines a course of action whose highest expression is war."[2]

Aestheticization may therefore lead not simply to a reduction in ontological meaning. When it works within the political arena, it may also lead to more sinister consequences. One of the first to theorize the aestheticization of politics was Walter Benjamin, who analyzed it in terms of fascism, which he was able to observe firsthand in post–World War I Germany. The rise of National Socialism, with the introduction of anti-Semitic legislation, deprived Benjamin of his livelihood as a journalist and broadcaster, forced him into exile, and ultimately cost him his life, when he committed suicide in 1940, on the Spanish border, frustrated in his attempt to flee Nazi-occupied France. But his experience of fascism also comes from his study of literary sources. His first literary engagement with the subject was his "Theories of German Fascism," a review of a volume of essays edited by Ernst Jünger, a veteran of World War I and renowned apologist for war. Here Benjamin detected an emerging theory of war that was "nothing other than an uninhibited translation of the principles of *l'art pour l'art* to war itself."[3]

Benjamin further develops this thesis in his essay "The Work of Art in the Age of Mechanical Reproduction."[4] Here he offers one of the most incisive critiques of the relationship between aesthetics and politics. Benjamin uses the extreme example of fascism to illustrate the problems that may occur when these two domains, which are viewed traditionally as having little in common, come together in that most "inherently contradictory juncture."[5] Fascism, in this sense, should be viewed not simply as a grotesque social phenomenon that was most fully realized in the first half of the twentieth century. Rather it should be recognized as an extreme moment that will always be prone to reappear whenever politics becomes aestheticized. To this end fascism can offer us some telling insights into the potential risks within our current aestheticized culture.

Within the context of Benjamin's essay it can be seen that a privileging of the image is itself not innocent. For Benjamin, there is a potential corruption within the process of aestheticization. It is not simply that aesthetics may dress up an unsavory political agenda and turn it into an intoxicating spectacle. Rather, with aestheticization a social and political displacement occurs whereby ethical concerns are replaced by aesthetic ones. A political agenda is judged, therefore, not according to its intrinsic ethical status but according to the appeal of its outward appearance. It could be argued that the mechanisms at play in the aestheticization of politics are more complex than Benjamin's analysis suggests. Politics and aesthetics are perhaps not quite the "contradictory" entities that he held them to be, in that within a certain constellation of circumstances the two may work in tandem. The aestheticization of politics, then, would involve a complex restructuring of ideological material in which politics and aesthetics would collude.[6] Yet Benjamin is no doubt correct to recognize the problems that may result from the aestheticization of politics, and while he himself might equally be accused of aestheticizing the world, his comments would appear to hold true for the world of aesthetics.

The overall effects of the aestheticization of politics are clear enough. The Nazis were fully aware of how to exploit this process, and it is perhaps no coincidence that it was an architect, Albert Speer, also armaments minister, who was the most successful at realizing its potential. In the spectacular rally that he masterminded in 1934 at the Zeppelin Field in Nuremburg, he turned a political rally into a work of art. This he achieved in part by involving the masses themselves in the spectacle, such that they were not only witnessing but also partaking of a highly orchestrated, mechanically precise work of art, and in part through the sublime stage effects that provided the backdrop to the spectacle. By arranging a battery of 130 anti-aircraft searchlights at intervals of 40 feet around the edge of the field and directing them up into the sky, Speer effected his famous "cathedral of light." The beams of the searchlights acted like giant, luminous columns. "It had the advantage of dramatizing the spectacle," Speer himself observed,

"while effectively drawing a veil over the not-so-attractive marching figures of paunchy party bureaucrats."[7] And it is in the sublime that art begins to align itself with the force and intensity of war. With the development of the sublime, art sets the scene for the aesthetic celebration of violence that underpinned fascist thinking. While fascism did not always operate within an aesthetic domain—there can be little of the aesthetic in the horror of Auschwitz—in its self-representation, and hence its self-justification and methods of propaganda, fascism exploited the aestheticization of politics.

The example that Benjamin actually uses to illustrate his argument is that of the Futurists in Italy. Just as Speer was to exploit the aestheticization of politics within a specifically political forum, so too the Futurists exploited it within an aesthetic domain. Benjamin in fact met the Futurist poet and propagandist Filippo Tommaso Marinetti in 1924. He describes him at the time as "quite a lad," and recounts how he performed a "noise poem" to great effect: "neighing, booming guns, rattling carts, machine-gun fire etc."[8] In his writings, however, Benjamin recognizes the sinister side of Marinetti's work, and Marinetti's manifesto provides Benjamin with material for analysis in his study of fascism in the "Work of Art" essay. Marinetti's aestheticized call for war gives an explicit formulation of the effects of the aestheticization of politics. The very putrefaction and destruction of war were celebrated by Marinetti as an aesthetic experience:

War is beautiful, because it establishes man's dominion over the subjugated machinery by means of gas masks, terrifying megaphones, flame throwers, and small tanks. War is beautiful because it initiates the dreamt-of metallization of the human body. War is beautiful because it enriches a flowering meadow with the fiery orchids of machine guns. War is beautiful because it combines the gun-fire, the cannonades, the cease-fire, the scents, and the stench of putrefaction into a symphony. War is beautiful because it creates new architecture, like that of the big tanks, the geometrical formation flights, the smoke spirals from burning villages, and many others. . . . Poets and artists of Futurism! . . . remember these principles of an aesthetic of war so that your struggle for a new literature and a new graphic art . . . may be illumined by them![9]

2.1 Albert Speer, "Cathedral of Light." Bayerische Staatsbibliothek München.

Benjamin is quite specific about how fascism arises. He sees the problem of modernity as that of trying to negotiate the rise of the proletarian masses within the existing property structure. One way to resolve the conflict is to resort to fascism, a form of politics that "attempts to organize the newly created proletarian masses without affecting the property structure which the masses aim to eliminate." Fascism therefore holds a particular appeal at the onset of modernity. And the "logical result" of fascism, for Benjamin, is the "introduction of aesthetics into political life." This has dire consequences: "All efforts to render politics aesthetic culminate in one thing: war. War and war alone can set a goal for mass movements on the largest scale while respecting the traditional property system."[10]

In modernity, according to Benjamin, technological production has increased enormously, but cannot be utilized in a natural manner because it is constrained by existing property structures. A society not "mature" enough to utilize that technology profitably will be plagued by unemployment and economic crisis. Fascism therefore offers a way out of this predicament by "unnaturally" releasing the pent-up emotions and drives through the medium of war. "'*Fiat ars—pereat mundus*,' says Fascism, and, as Marinetti admits, expects war to supply the artistic gratification of a sense perception that has been changed by technology."[11] It is precisely by rendering war a spectacle and taking delight in the aesthetic gratification of destruction that fascism offers such appeal within a world that has become radically self-alienated. In this fetishizing of the surface, deeper ontological questions—the horror and inhumanity of war—come to be glossed over. In the intoxication of the moment, social and political realities are overlooked. In the aesthetic celebration of war, the aestheticization of politics realizes its full, disturbing potential.

The Aestheticization of Architecture

Events were to prove Benjamin all too accurate concerning the inevitable consequence of the aestheticization of politics. At the other end of the twentieth century, however, we might perhaps reevaluate his conclusion amid the saturation of images in our present media society. In an era when, as Baudrillard has observed, everything has been transported into the realm of the aesthetic, politics themselves have become aestheticized across the whole spectrum from left to right. We might therefore recognize that while this process may indeed culminate in war, it may equally lead to a dilution, a reduction of the political to the level of image. The problem, then, of the aestheticization of politics becomes particularly acute in an age of aestheticization, when war may be reduced to a mere image. It is a problem, as Bernard Tschumi has observed, that extends to the very heart of our architectural culture.

A general form of aestheticization has indeed taken place, conveyed by the media. Just as Stealth Bombers are aestheticised on the televised Saudi Arabian sunset, just as sex is aestheticised in advertising, so all of culture—and of course this includes architecture—is now aestheticised. "Xeroxised." Furthermore the simultaneous presentation of these images leads to a reduction of history to simultaneous images: not only those of the Gulf War interspersed with basketball games and advertisements, but also those of our architectural magazines and, ultimately, those of our cities.[12]

The consequences of this are profound. For the reduction in depth induced by this process of aestheticization ensures that the Gulf War is treated at the same level as a basketball match. As Baudrillard has pointed out infamously, "The Gulf War did not take place."[13] It is not simply that in an age of high-tech gadgetry and sophisticated electronic systems the military does not experience a real war, and that the very predictability of the outcome and the relative absence of actual armed conflict create what is essentially a nonwar. Rather, the simulation of the actual events by the media conspires to make this a virtual war. In a culture of simulation—a TV world of popcorn, microwaved dinners, and home movies—we have lost our capacity to grasp the reality of war. The horror of war is consumed as though it were a horror movie, and the news flash from the front line competes against serialized soap operas for prime time audience ratings. In this aestheticized world of appearances, the Gulf War is rinsed of its ontological reality as a war to

2.2 F-117 Stealth fighter bomber. Grazia Neri.

2.3 Hawk surface-to-air missiles. Grazia Neri.

2.4 Night sky over Baghdad, Iraq, January 16, 1991. Grazia Neri.

become a hyperreal form of entertainment. And it is in this "sacred horizon of appearances" that a machinery of death—the Stealth bomber—can seem so seductive against the pink and orange hues of the Saudi Arabian sunset.

All this might lead us to reconsider whether in fact these two manifestations of the aestheticization of politics—the fascism addressed by Benjamin, and the more diluted politics of the image today—might have something in common. For the aestheticization of politics is not simply a displacement of the political by the aesthetic but a reconfiguration of their relationship, in which the two collude in an often complex fashion. Could it be, then, that both forms of the aestheticization of politics contribute to a similar end, and that there is a deeply reactionary program lurking beneath *both* projects? Might not fascism, with its subtle intertwining of the political and the aesthetic, indeed have some insights to offer regarding the status of the political today, and most especially in a discipline such as architecture in which the image plays such a crucial role? And if what is at risk is the possibility of fascism, how might we see this question borne out in the practice of architecture?

From a historical perspective there can be little doubt that architecture has played an important role in totalitarian regimes. Ceausescu, no less than Hitler, Stalin, and Mussolini before him, employed architecture as a form of "word in stone." Less obvious, perhaps, but equally significant is the way in which architecture has developed certain fascistic tendencies in more commonplace situations. And these incidents are all the more insidious precisely because they do not declare themselves in so obvious a fashion.

The most disturbing question, therefore, is not how architecture might be appropriated and exploited by various fascistic regimes, but how architectural culture might itself register a certain fascistic impulse. Here fascism must be understood not in its specific historical sense, but in the generic sense of the excessive use or abuse of any form of power, whether by the left or the right. Certainly, there are remarkable parallels to be drawn between images of dictators, such as

Ceausescu or Hitler, inspecting architectural models, and those of architects themselves in similar situations. Architectural issues with important social and political ramifications are all too often decided on solely aesthetic grounds. To this extent the insensitivity of the dictator forcing a road through a highly populated neighborhood, with little concern for the social and political consequences, is often matched by the insensitivity of the architect who engages in a curious power game through the vicarious use of architectural models. The sheer difference in scale between architects and their models allows them to assume a Gulliver-like position of authority vis-à-vis the actual site of their proposals. Entire districts may be erased at the cut of a scalpel in an exercise that often operates merely at the level of the aesthetic. The consequence of this, one might suppose, is not simply that within every fascist dictator there is a potential architect, but also that within every architect there is a potential fascist.

Benjamin himself depicts the fascist as the "pilot of a single airplane full of gas bombs . . . in his lofty solitude, alone with himself and his God." His power is absolute: "and wherever he puts his signature, no more grass will grow."[14] It is in the context of contemporary computerized military hardware, of pilots abstracted from their targets on the ground, desensitized within their own technological bubble, that we can begin to trace parallels with our architects of today. For it is not only the mediation of the computer screen and the inculcation of design ideology that has often distanced architects from everyday life; the whole aestheticization of the discourse of architecture has anaesthetized them, left them trapped within their aesthetic cocoons, such that even destruction might be treated at the level of the aesthetic.

The spirit of the Futurists, it would seem, is echoed in the work of Lebbeus Woods, who in his book *War and Architecture* clearly finds the death and destruction in Sarajevo a deeply aesthetic experience. "War is architecture, and architecture is war!" he proclaims.[15] What is most alarming about this equation of architecture with war is not the attempt to see architecture as a form of war, for inevitably architecture will involve some warlike destruction, in that the very process of

2.5 Lebbeus Woods, study for Sarajevo. Woods, *War and Architecture*, p. 13.

construction presupposes the destruction of whatever had previously belonged to the site. It is, rather, the tendency to see war as a form of architecture. The destruction of the physical fabric of Sarajevo provides the aesthetic impetus for new forms of architecture, such as the "injection," the "scar," and the "scab," terms that belong to a discourse of mutilated bodies. These forms accept the destroyed condition of the buildings and incorporate it into their aesthetic. The "injection" is a structure "injected" into spaces left void by destruction. The structure does not fit exactly, but leaves a gap between the old and the new. The "scab" is a new construction that "shields an exposed interior space or void, protecting it during its subsequent transformations."[16] The "scar" meanwhile is a "deeper level of construction" that "fuses the new and the old, reconciling, coalescing them, without compromising either one in the name of a contextual or other form of unity."[17] These forms, then, are generated in response to the destruction of the buildings, but, more importantly, in their jagged, torn aesthetic they complement and draw inspiration from the forms of mutilated buildings. As such they constitute an aesthetic celebration of destruction.

"I am at war," Woods claims, "with my time, with history, with all authority that resides in fixed and frightened forms."[18] Behind a veneer of sympathetic rhetoric, expressing concern for the future of Sarajevo and empathy for its condition, Woods seemingly fails to acknowledge the aestheticization that lies at the heart of his project, a condition that is exacerbated by his proposed architectural solutions. Here the lack of any rigorously worked-through social and political agenda lends his techno-architecture an air of science fiction, thereby increasing the distance between his seductive images and the actual reality of life on the streets of Sarajevo. What is more, the very fetishization of technology in his project further abstracts the work from its social context. Meanwhile, in place of any real consideration of the politics of use of the proposed buildings and their spatial practices, Woods offers postmodern slogans of "hybridity" and "heterarchy," which are somehow championed as the antidote to hierarchical, organized war, under the questionable premise that since war has to be organized, whatever counters the hierarchical may somehow prevent war:

2.6 Lebbeus Woods, study for Sarajevo. Woods, *War and Architecture,* p. 15.

Ragged tears in walls, roofs, and floor structures created by explosions and fires are complex forms and figurations, unique in their history and meaning. No two are alike, yet they all share a common aspect: they have resulted from the unpredictable effects of forces released in the calculated risks of war. They are the beginnings of new ways of thinking, living and shaping space, arising from individuality and invention. From them a heterarchical community can be formed, one that precludes the hierarchical basis for organized violence and war.[19]

Woods is not alone, of course, in his assumption that architectural form can somehow determine human behavior, and that good design can lead to a better world. This is an assumption—a myth—written into the whole history of architectural discourse. But the relationship between his architectural forms and the liberal politics of the "free-spaces" that he espouses is an issue not confronted. For Woods it is enough to propose "freespaces"—"forms . . . which do not invite occu-pation with the old paraphernalia of living, the old ways of living and thinking." Instead they offer a "dense matrix of new conditions."[20]

If, however, we are to believe Michel Foucault, architectural form in itself cannot determine these conditions. In his discussion of Bentham's panopticon, Foucault offers some clear and incisive com-ments on the link between architecture and a politics of use.[21] The panopticon consists of several stories of cells arranged radially around a central control tower. This latter incorporates blinds and other devices to ensure that the prisoners in the cells are unsure whether or not they are being observed, while the guards themselves have a clear view into each of the cells. The architectural form, in other words, facilitates the efficient monitoring of the prisoners. It is a principle that has been used in libraries and other facilities with central control posts, and one that also extends into more recent forms of surveillance, such as remote-control cameras. The very architectural layout of the panopticon affords various techniques of control, which, Foucault thought, would in themselves assure almost automatically the subjection and the subjec-tification of the inmates.

Foucault revisits the example of the panopticon in a subsequent interview, "Space, Knowledge, Power." Here he stresses that it is not the architectural form in itself which might act as a force of liberation or control. "I think that it can never be inherent in the structure of things to guarantee the exercise of freedom. The guarantee of freedom is freedom."[22] All that architectural form can hope to achieve is to hinder or prevent a certain politics of use. Architectural form in itself cannot be liberating, although it can produce "positive effects" when the "liberating intentions of the architect" coincide with "the real practice of people in the exercise of their freedom."[23] In the case of the panopticon, then, it is not the architectural form that conditions behavior, but the power differential between guard and prisoners. The efficient layout of the architecture merely supports the exercise of this power. Foucault thereby makes a crucial observation on the capacity for architecture to influence human behavior.

Returning to Woods, it is clear that he is naïve to expect his "freespaces" to promote a liberal politics, since architectural form in itself cannot determine any particular politics of use. All that architecture can do is offer spaces that might—at best—"invite" certain spatial practices. Yet Woods has not investigated the spatial practices of a liberal society, nor what architectural forms might best accommodate those practices. His suggestions remain locked within an aesthetics of form. The work of Woods on Sarajevo can therefore be seen as an aestheticization of the world. Not only have the deeply political questions of reuse of damaged buildings been transported into the realm of architectural aesthetics, but the whole imagery of war-torn buildings has been appropriated as a point of departure for a new aestheticized view of the world. The warnings of Walter Benjamin, it seems, have not been heeded. Nowhere are the problems of aestheticization more pertinent than here in this superficial fetishization of the image of war.

If the destruction in Sarajevo can provide the starting point for a design aesthetic, and images of the Gulf War can be treated on the same level as basketball matches and advertisements, what hope is there for any meaningful discourse of architecture? The world has become aestheticized and anaesthetized, emptied of all content. And nowhere is this condition more marked, it would seem, than in the glossy pages of our architectural magazines and the fashion-conscious domains of our schools of architecture.

3

THE AESTHETICS OF INTOXICATION

German sociologist and philosopher Georg Simmel was quick to associate new patterns of conscious behavior with the environmental landscape of modernity. In his essay "The Metropolis and Mental Life" (1903), Simmel offers us one of the most penetrating insights into the life of the modernist metropolitan individual. "The psychological foundation upon which the metropolitan individuality is erected," he observes, "is the intensification of emotional life due to the swift and continuous shift of external and internal stimuli."[1] In contrast to those who lived in the towns or countryside, where life is characterized by a "slower, more habitual, more smoothly flowing rhythm," the metropolitan individual has to accommodate and register the rapid bombardment of stimuli within the city, where even the crossing of the road would fray the nerves. The registering of the fragmentary and irregular impulses of city life has a marked impact on the psychological outlook of the metropolitan type. Whereas the steady and familiar patterns of rural life could be accommodated with little mental effort, the "rapid telescoping of changing images" in the city, the "pronounced differences within what is grasped at a single glance, and the unexpectedness of violent stimuli" call for a greater expenditure of mental energy. And whereas rural life somehow appeals "at a more unconscious level" to feelings and emotional relationships, metropolitan life could best be grasped at an abstracted, intellectual level. Accordingly, Simmel presents a model of the modern metropolitan type as one whose intellectualized and unemotional patterns of behavior within the capitalist metropolis match the movement of capitalism itself. The metropolitan individual has developed, for Simmel, an abstracted, disinterested form of movement that echoes the circulation of money.

Central to Simmel's thesis is the concept of the blasé outlook. The modern metropolitan individual has to develop a defense mechanism against the overstimulation of mental life in the city, and the blasé outlook is both a product of and a defense against this condition. The blasé outlook, for Simmel, "is at first the consequence of those rapidly shifting stimulations of the nerves which are thrown together in all their contrasts and from which it seems to us the intensification of metropolitan intellectuality seems to be derived."[2]

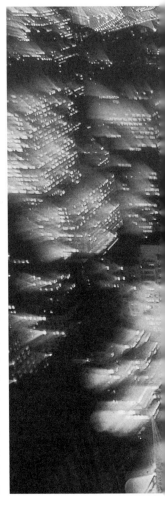

Just as an immoderately sensuous life makes one blasé because it stimulates the nerves to their utmost reactivity until they finally can no longer produce any reaction at all, so, less harmful stimuli, through the rapidity and the contradictoriness of their shifts, force the nerves to make such violent responses, tear them about so brutally that they exhaust their last reserves of strength and, remaining in the same milieu, do not have the time for new reserves to form.[3]

To become blasé therefore constitutes an inability to react sufficiently to the mental impulses of the city. But the crucial point is that this condition is essentially a defensive one. By underreacting to external stimuli, the metropolitan individual develops a form of defensive cocoon against overstimulation. The blasé outlook reveals how that individual has learned to survive within the conditions of the modern metropolis. The blasé attitude is therefore an adaptive phenomenon "in which the nerves reveal their final possibility for adjusting themselves to the content and the form of metropolitan life by renouncing the response to them."[4]

Similar themes might be found in the work of Walter Benjamin, who looks at the modern metropolitan type through the lens of Charles Baudelaire. Indeed it was Baudelaire who had articulated, long before Simmel, the trancelike state that lay at the basis of the blasé individual.

3.1 Manhattan. Francisco Hidalgo.

Baudelaire, who had himself experimented with drugs of various kinds, presents life in the metropolis as a narcoticlike trance, and it is a life shrouded in a mythic dimension. For Baudelaire, as Benjamin observes, the metropolis was the mesmerizing site of a religious intoxication.[5]

The Narcotics of the City

The Surrealists had likewise recognized the intoxicating nature of the metropolis. For them the city was above all an enchanting dreamscape that fired and fueled the imagination. The very cacophony of the city with its blaring horns and flashing neon lights—the fragmentary, kaleidoscopic impulses of the modern metropolis—provided them with a continual source of stimulation and intoxication. This they achieved by raising their aesthetic consciousness and deliberately playing upon the phenomenon that Simmel had observed. Their receptivity to the sensory stimulation of the city induced a form of narcotic trance that allowed one to "surrender oneself to such enticements, to roam the enchanted metropolis in pursuit of desire and distraction."[6]

While the Surrealists explored the potential of alcohol and drugs as a means of enhancing their perception of the city, Surrealism itself could open them to that "intoxication." "Today I bring you a narcotic originating at the limits of consciousness, at the very edge of the abyss," writes Louis Aragon. "This is the entrance to the realms of the instantaneous, the world of snapshot."[7] It is under the narcotic of Surrealism that Aragon entreats readers "without even an instrument in your hands . . . [to] find yourselves evoking the hitherto incomplete gamut of [the hashish eaters'] pleasures . . . casting a spell over yourselves by piercing the mortal cross-piece of your heart not with a pin but with an enchanting image." And it was under such an intoxication that Aragon himself conceived of his mythology of the modern: "Walking tipsily among so many divine concretions . . . I set about forming the idea of a mythology in motion. It was more accurate to call it a mythology of the modern. And it was under that name that I conceived it."[8]

In this spirit of abandonment the world could become mytholo-
gized, and even the most technical and seemingly rational of objects
could be transformed into mythic creatures. For Aragon even the modern petrol pump could metamorphose into some mythic form:

Painted brightly with English or invented names, possessing just one long,
supple arm, a luminous faceless head, a single foot and a numbered wheel in
the belly, the petrol pumps sometimes take on the appearance of the divinities
of Egypt or of those cannibal tribes which worship war and war alone. O
Texaco motor oil, Esso, Shell, great inscriptions of human potentiality, soon
shall we cross ourselves before your fountains, and the youngest among us will
perish from having contemplated their nymphs in naptha.[9]

For the Surrealists, as for Baudelaire, the metropolis was the source
of perpetual intoxication. It had a narcotic effect, the capacity to induce
a blasé attitude in the individual. And like Simmel, Baudelaire based
this condition on the principle of the "shock." As Benjamin observed,
modernity for Baudelaire is characterized by sudden sharp movements
such as the triggering of the shutter in the camera, and other visual
equivalents:

Tactile experiences of this kind were joined by optic ones, such as are supplied
by the advertising pages of a newspaper or the traffic of a big city. Moving
through this traffic involves the individual in a series of shocks or collisions.
At dangerous crossings, nervous impulses flow through him in rapid succes-
sion, like the energy from a battery. Baudelaire speaks of a man who plunges
into the crowd, as into a reservoir of electric energy. Circumscribing the experience of the shock, he calls this man "a kaleidoscope equipped with consciousness."[10]

Benjamin picks up on these themes in Baudelaire. He acknowledges the appeal of the metropolis for the Surrealists, and while he is
critical of the "mythology of the modern" that Aragon and others
espoused, he claims—rather surprisingly—to recognize an emancipa-
tory potential in Surrealism through what he terms the "dialectics of
intoxication." In this sense, somewhat paradoxically, the intoxication of
the city might provide a form of "profane illumination," a momentary
glimpse of the reality behind the myth.[11] The problem of modernity,

for Benjamin, is precisely that of myth, as understood within the context of the dialectic of the Enlightenment, where myth and rationality comprised the two opposite poles of Enlightenment culture held in a reciprocal tension. Myth—that magical "other" to Enlightenment rationality—constituted a form of false consciousness. It effectively obscured reality. While modernity has generally been viewed as the obviation of myth, the disenchantment of the world, the modern metropolis for Benjamin is entangled with myth, a form of dreamworld, the intoxicating site of the phantasmagoric, the kaleidoscopic, and the cacophonous. The modern metropolis does not escape myth but is precisely *enslaved* by myth, a myth that has adopted new guises in the supposedly progressive, fashionable world of the commodity. Thus the very abstraction of modern manufacturing allows its products to appear to be "conjured up"—as if by magic—to constitute the phantasmagoria of this dreamworld. This process is fueled by the fashion system, "the always-the-same dressed up as the ever-new."[12] Fashion, for Benjamin, acts as a "tireless agent" that contributes to the false consciousness of this dreamworld. All this is veiled by the deceptive doctrine of progress that underpins modern existence and masks the continuing barbarity of history. "There is no document of civilization," as Benjamin notes, "which is not at the same time a document of barbarism."[13]

If the modern metropolis is enshrouded in myth, as if by some form of false consciousness, for Benjamin it is the task of the responsible individual to see through this myth—to demythologize the world. It is here that Surrealism may hold some revolutionary potential. Even though Surrealism would itself appear to be based on the principle of myth, it contains the potential for political change through its "profane illumination" which, for Benjamin, could penetrate this layer of myth. Through a "dialectics of intoxication," which was not dependent on narcotics but bore similar characteristics, the "profane illumination" offered a flashlike glimpse of a world free of myth. "The true, creative overcoming of religious illumination certainly does not lie in narcotics," writes Benjamin. "It resides in a profane illumination, a materialist, anthropological inspiration, to which hashish, opium, or whatever else can give an introductory lesson."[14] Surrealism therefore held the promise of emancipation through its revolutionary insights. "To win the energies of intoxication for the revolution": this was for Benjamin the "most particular task" of Surrealism.[15]

Likewise Benjamin recognized the narcotic effect of the city. In the swirling crowds of the modern metropolis the subject, for Benjamin, becomes enveloped in a form of aesthetic cocoon as though drugged. Benjamin's primary subject is the flaneur, the urban dawdler, who, like the prostitute and the ragpicker, inhabits the left-over spaces, like the arcades, at the threshold of modernity, as one era passes into the next. The flaneur, then, is quite historically specific. And if, for Benjamin, it is in their obsolescence that objects reveal their potential, so the flaneur, the last gasp of a previous order, comes to embody the prehistory of the modern. The flaneur in Benjamin, this disinterested observer, famed for taking tortoises for walks and other strategies aimed at resisting the onslaught of the modern world, yet equally content to sell his wares in the modern marketplace, has certain similarities with the blasé individual in Simmel's writing. The flaneur may indeed be blasé, but unlike Simmel's blasé individual he is not a creature of the crowd. The flaneur is a student of modern life, more at home observing the crowd from the window of some café. But equally the flaneur may become intoxicated by the crowd and swept up blissfully by it, like a commodity enveloped in a stream of customers:

The crowd is not only the newest asylum of outlaws; it is also the latest narcotic for those abandoned. The *flâneur* is someone abandoned in the crowd. In this he shares the situation of the commodity. He is not aware of this special situation, but this does not diminish its effect on him and it permeates him blissfully like a narcotic that can compensate him for many humiliations. The intoxication to which the *flâneur* surrenders is the intoxication of the commodity around which surges the stream of customers.[16]

It is perhaps no coincidence that Benjamin himself experimented in taking drugs as a means of engaging with the city. In "Hashish in Marseilles" he reports how, under the effects of hashish, "space can expand, the ground tilt steeply, atmospheric senses occur: vapor, an opaque heaviness of the air; colors grow brighter, more luminous; objects more beautiful."[17] The narcotic heightens Benjamin's sensitivity to everything around him, to the point where he feels as though a shadow falling on a piece of paper threatens to harm it.[18] At the same time it distances him from reality and distorts his experience of the city, so that the blaring of car horns is mistaken for a brass band. It is as though the intoxication allows him to make sense of the fragmentary impulses of the city.[19] The city becomes a comforting, almost religious fiction, so that Benjamin can compare the Surrealist experience of the city with the "opium" of religion.[20]

What Benjamin adds to the accounts of the modern metropolis in Simmel, Baudelaire, Aragon, and others is a certain psychoanalytic dimension. While recognizing similar symptoms, Benjamin offers a somewhat different analysis. While Simmel describes the blasé individual in straightforwardly neurological terms, as someone whose nerve endings had been desensitized by overstimulation, in Benjamin's account the *mind* is what is anaesthetized by the continual shocks of contemporary existence.[21]

The Shock of the Modern

Certainly, for Benjamin, it is shock that lies at the heart of modern existence, where technology not only creates an environment fundamentally different from any previous era but also conditions human behavior and engenders a predominant mental outlook. For Benjamin, the human psyche is in essence an organic mechanism, which is constantly adapting to its physical surroundings. This adaptation has to be seen as a defensive mechanism predicated on survival. The human being, in this sense, is like a chameleon, governed by an instinctual urge to find similarities in the external environment, and, where none exist, to adapt itself to that environment. The term that Benjamin uses for this process is *mimesis*. Through the mimetic impulse the human being seeks to replicate aspects of the external world. This process appears to be governed by the death instinct—the urge to be at one with the environment—but is premised on survival and not on death.[22] Hence we might recognize a sacrificial theme in mimesis. For just as sacrifice in religious terms aims to continue life through death—by in effect transcending death—so the chameleonlike instinct at the heart of mimesis uses mimicry as a mechanism of survival. This can be recognized when humans, like so many animals, freeze when confronted with a life-threatening situation. The very process of freezing—of adopting a life-less form—is a mechanism of feigning death for the sake of survival. By appearing inert, a creature attempts to camouflage itself and blend in with its surroundings, as though it were invisible.

This principle, for Benjamin, underpins all human activity. The mimetic principle would therefore dictate that human beings are constantly adapting to their surroundings. The fragmentary impulses of the city, the jolting, jarring experiences of modern life, would be replicated in human beings' own behavior. Humans would develop reflexes and responses to match those of their external environment. For Benjamin, the archetypal example of this could be found in crowd behavior. In Poe's tale of the man in the crowd, Benjamin notes how the individual, when jostled, would bow profusely to the jostlers like some form of automaton.[23] It is in this very gesture, a gesture as empty as the token smile, that Benjamin recognizes the essence of modernity.

Through such abstracted patterns of behavior, articulated so clearly in Fritz Lang's film *Metropolis,* human beings have taken on some of the attributes of machines. The German architect and social theorist Siegfried Kracauer makes an explicit comparison between the mechanized labor practices of modernity and the corresponding aesthetic practices. In his analysis of the Tiller Girls dance troupe he offers an incisive account of how the depersonalized patterns of their dance routines are emblematic of the abstract rationality that pervades culture at large:

Everyone does his or her task on the conveyor belt, performing a partial function without grasping the totality. . . . Like the pattern in the stadium, the organization . . . is conceived according to rational principles which the Taylor system merely pushes to their ultimate conclusion. The hands in the factory correspond to the legs of the Tiller Girls. . . . The mass ornament is the aesthetic reflex of the rationality to which the prevailing economic system aspires.[24]

For Benjamin, these patterns are a mechanism of survival in an age dominated by the jolting, jarring repetitive action of the machine. Benjamin makes his comparison quite specific: the mechanization of human movement replicates the movement of the machine. "The shock experience which the passerby has in the crowd," he notes, "corresponds to what the worker 'experiences' by his machine." He adds that Baudelaire had been "captivated by a process whereby the reflecting mechanism which the machine sets off in the workman can be studied closely, as in a mirror, in the idler."[25] But what makes Benjamin's analysis of modern life so telling is the psychological account he offers of this process, an account that is based on the work of Sigmund Freud:

For a living organism, protection against stimuli is an almost more important function than the reception of stimuli: the protective shield is equipped with its own store of energy and must above all strive to conserve the special forms of energy operating in it against the effects of the excessive energies at work in the external world.[26]

Here Benjamin is making an explicit comparison between Proust's *mémoire involontaire*—involuntary memory—and Freud's notion of consciousness, as articulated in *Beyond the Pleasure Principle*. Benjamin notes the opposition between the two. *Mémoire involontaire* depends on an event not entering consciousness, which leads him to conclude that consciousness serves as a reservoir of energy to dampen the energies outside, and therefore to act as a protection against stimuli.

The threat from these energies is one of shock. The more readily consciousness registers these shocks, the less likely they are to have a traumatic effect. Psychoanalytic theory strives to understand the nature of these traumatic shocks, "on the basis of their breaking through the protective shield against stimuli."[27]

Freud situates the protective shield within "wakeful consciousness," located in part of the cortex that is "so blown apart by the effect of the stimulus" that it offers "the most favorable situation for the reception of stimuli."[28] By "parrying" the shock, consciousness prevents it from entering into the realm of experience and being retained within the memory. Consciousness therefore acts as a form of shock absorber, which limits the long-term damage of the shock by isolating it within a particular moment: "The greater the share of the shock factor in particular impressions, the more constantly consciousness has to be alert as a screen against stimuli; the more efficiently it does so, the less do these impressions enter experience *(Erfahrung),* tending to remain in the sphere of a certain hour of one's life *(Erlebnis)*."[29] In presenting consciousness as though it were some form of "fencer" attempting to "parry" the shocks of modern existence, Benjamin adopted an image used by Baudelaire to represent contact with the metropolitan masses: "the blows he deals are designed to open a path through the crowd for him."[30]

It is in this context that we might understand the role of consciousness, for Benjamin, in dealing with the shock of the aesthetic. What have to be "parried" by the modern metropolitan individual are not so much the masses in the street as the fragmentary, kaleidoscopic sensations of the metropolis—the neon lighting, the flashing lights and blaring horns, the intoxicating cacophony of the street. These bring about the numbing effect of the modern metropolis, where neon advertisements "sink into the mind," as Siegfried Kracauer observes, leaving a "reddish gleam that lingers . . . like a cloak over one's thoughts."[31]

Aesthetics and Anaesthetics

Benjamin himself focuses on the phantasmagoria of nineteenth-century Paris in his analysis of this condition, as Buck-Morss notes. The original phantasmagoria took the form of the private fantasy worlds of bourgeois interiors with their luxurious display of furnishings. The principle then extended to the shop windows of the arcades, and thence to the "panoramas and dioramas that engulfed the viewer in a simulated total environment-in-miniature" and finally to the world's fairs, "which expanded this phantasmagoric principle to areas the size of small cities."[32]

It is the principle of the phantasmagoria, the sensory bombardment of techno-aesthetics, that illustrates the potential of the aesthetic
for inducing a form of anaesthesia. The emphasis on visual display over-
whelms and intoxicates the viewer. The aesthetic experience thus serves
as a form of narcotic: "It has the effect of anaesthetizing the organism,
not through numbing, but through flooding the senses. These stimu-
lated sensoria alter consciousness, much like a drug, but they do so
through sensory distraction rather than chemical alteration."[33]

The intoxication of the aesthetic may therefore anaesthetize the
subject. The paradox of all this, as Buck-Morss observes, is that the
term "aesthetic" is seemingly associated with its opposite, "anaesthetic."
Some explanation might be found in the way the term *aesthetic* has
changed and lost its original meaning. The ancient Greek term, *aesthe-
sis,* refers not to abstract theories of beauty but to sensory perceptions.[34]
It involves a heightening of feelings and emotions and an awakening of
the senses, the very opposite of "anaesthetics." This original meaning is
precisely what is evoked here. The process of aestheticization heightens
awareness toward sensory stimuli. This in turn triggers a compen-
satory anaesthetization as a protection against overstimulation.
Anaesthetization therefore works in tandem with aestheticization; the
one feeds into the other. Just as hashish increases Benjamin's aesthetic
awareness of the city of Marseilles, so too the bombardment of images
may prove to have a narcotic effect, heightening one's aesthetic receptivity to further visual stimulation. But this flooding of the senses in
one domain blots out the reception of impulses in another. The raising
of one's consciousness of sensory matters—smell, taste, touch, sound,
and appearance—allows a corresponding indifference to descend like a
blanket over all else. The process generates its own womblike sensory
cocoon around the individual, a semipermeable membrane that ensures
a state of constant gratification by filtering out all that is undesirable.
To aestheticize is therefore to sink blissfully into an intoxicating stupor
that serves to cushion the individual from the world outside like some
alcoholic haze.

The response that Simmel describes is a largely involuntary one,
brought on by the conditions of the modern metropolis. For it is the

kaleidoscopic and fragmentary impulses of modern life that engender the blasé attitude, as the nerves attempt to defend themselves. But the response that Benjamin describes depends upon a certain receptivity toward those conditions. For those not disposed to such an outlook, the city may be the site of irritation and annoyance. Indeed Benjamin's own account is a receptive, largely aesthetic one—the view from a café, rather than from the factory floor. Crucially, then, aestheticization depends upon an active engagement on the part of the viewer, and a deliberate raising of one's aesthetic awareness.

This is precisely the sort of outlook common among those who work within the realm of visual images. Good design obviously depends upon a strong sense of visual awareness, but this emphasis on the image has certain negative consequences; and it is in a discipline like architecture, which is so directly involved with social concerns, that these negative consequences are likely to be most keenly experienced. The aestheticization of the world induces a form of numbness. It reduces any notion of pain to the level of the seductive image. What is at risk in this process of aestheticization is that political and social content may be subsumed, absorbed, and denied.[35] The seduction of the image works against any underlying sense of social commitment. Architecture is potentially compromised within this aestheticized realm. Architects, it would seem, are particularly susceptible to an aesthetic that fetishizes the ephemeral image, the surface membrane. The world becomes aestheticized and anaesthetized. In the intoxicating world of the image, the aesthetics of architecture threaten to become the *ana*esthetics of architecture.

The Intoxication of the Aesthetic

One of the realms in which the links between intoxication and the aesthetic have been exploited most successfully has been advertising. What this reveals most clearly is that advertising relies upon a certain aesthetics of intoxication. For advertising does not simply depend upon a set of glamorous associations in order to sell a product—as in the often exploitative use of women in car advertisements. Rather it plays upon a certain narcotic quality within the aesthetic itself. It is precisely the aesthetic that operates as a form of drug to intoxicate and entice the viewer.

Nowhere is this more clearly demonstrated than in advertisements for alcohol and other forms of narcotic, such as cigarettes. A constant trope in this form of advertising is an almost hyperreal displacement into a different world. An advertisement for Marlboro cigarettes, for example, seeks to persuade viewers that by smoking that particular brand, they will be transported into "Marlboro country," the rough barren landscape of the wild west. Likewise an advertisement for Southern Comfort bourbon whiskey will invariably draw upon the exotic, mysterious world of the deep South. By drinking the product, it is suggested, one might be transported to the intoxicating world of New Orleans. Alcohol is invariably presented as though it offers some form of ecstatic escapism—a displacement of the mind from the body—and it is precisely the narcotic quality of the advertising image that feeds this impression.

One of the most successful advertisements from this point of view has been a recent commercial for Bacardi rum by Gray Advertising. The commercial opens with a voice-over with a London cockney accent describing a seemingly humdrum night at the pub, with phrases such as: "Peckham on a Monday night," "The Dog 'n' Duck down the High Street," "Aunty Beryl," and "Catching the last bus home." This voice-over is intended to evoke an all too familiar set of images from everyday life in Britain, but what is remarkable is the contrast it establishes with the accompanying visual images. These depict glamorous scenes from a desert island. The visual images contrast sharply with the all too unglamorous world of inner London, and yet, strikingly, they are precisely connected with it.

The voice-over "Peckham on a Monday night," which for many people would summon up the grim reality of a traffic-congested part of inner London at the start of the working week, is paired with an image of a palm-fringed, sun-drenched beach lapped by the waters of an azure-blue sea. "The Dog 'n' Duck down the High Street," which again

3.2 Bacardi commercial, "Peckham on a Monday night." Gray Advertising.

would evoke an all too stuffy, smoke-filled pub on a busy main road, is linked with a bar on that beach, where suntanned customers in colorful beachwear sip cocktails cooled by a gentle breeze blowing in from the sea. "Aunty Beryl," who would conjure up for many a familiar, slightly aging barmaid—no doubt with a fuller figure—becomes a beautiful, lithe, exotic young lady with dark, mysterious eyes. There is deliberate irony at play here. The young woman is described as "Aunty Beryl" precisely because she is not "Aunty Beryl." Meanwhile "Catching the last bus home," which might well evoke a rather mundane trip on a double-decker bus through the diesel fumes of London traffic, turns into a group of young men in light linen suits running down a jetty and leaping into a speedboat. The contrast between the voice-over with the London cockney accent and the exotic beach images could not be greater.

3.3 Bacardi commercial, "The Dog 'n' Duck down the High Street." Gray Advertising.

3.4 Bacardi commercial, "Aunty Beryl." Gray Advertising.

3.5 Bacardi commercial, "Catching the last bus home." Gray Advertising.

It is here that the subtlety of this commercial becomes most apparent. For it is by exposing and playing upon the contrast between the real and the imaginary that the commercial achieves its force. The ecstatic displacement suggested by the contrast between the voice-over and the images is one that is replicated—so the viewer is led to believe—by Bacardi rum. The commercial plays upon a certain narcotic quality in the drink itself. It presents Bacardi as though drinking it will transport you out of the grim reality of the local pub and into the exotic utopia of some desert island. But the commercial is all the more effective for constantly reminding the viewer of the real world. In some senses, then, the viewer remains within the actual space of the real, but is transported emotionally out of that space—as though in some mode of ecstasy—into a paradisaic world beyond. The narcotic quality of the drink will allow you to escape the humdrum world of everyday life.

What also makes this particular commercial so relevant to the present discussion is the way in which it was exploited by an architectural firm, T P Bennett Associates, who have adapted it for their own recruitment advertisement, openly playing upon its central theme. The Bacardi commercial is cleverly reappropriated for different ends. The second advertisement adopts the voice-over slogans as part of its text, but replaces the images of the exotic utopia by images of the designer world of an architectural office. What is significant here is that this second advert does not need to resort to the utopian escapism of the Bacardi advert. "Peckham on a Monday night," far from being transformed into its opposite—the remote idyll of an island paradise—remains within the space of London and is actually represented by an image of the most frenetic part of the city. While Peckham itself is a suburb trapped within the vast conurbation of greater London, the advert shows an image of central London, where the traffic is all the more busy and the sensory bombardment all the more intense. One is reminded of Simmel's comments on the fragmentary, kaleidoscopic impulses of the city that fray the nerve endings of modern metropolitan individuals, rendering them blasé. The very "shock" of the modern world is deliberately played upon here in order to induce an anaesthetized, narcotic condition.

3.6 Recruitment advertisement, T P Bennett Associates.

3.7 Recruitment advertisement, "Peckham on a Monday night." T P Bennett Associates.

3.8 Recruitment advertisement, "The Dog 'n' Duck down the High Street." T P Bennett Associates.

3.9 Recruitment advertisement, "Next door's loft conversion." T P Bennett Associates.

3.10 Recruitment advertisement, "Aunty Beryl." T P Bennett Associates.

This aestheticized image of the city is reinforced by others. Emblems of everyday life such as "The Dog 'n' Duck down the High Street" and "Next door's loft conversion" are represented as seductive images of high-tech buildings. The suggestion is that the high-tech bar in "The Dog 'n' Duck down the High Street" is an equivalent to the bar on the palm-fringed beach in the Bacardi commercial. In other words, their *effects* are similar. "Aunty Beryl" remains an exotic, beautiful young lady, but she is displaced from a desert island to behind a reception desk. The palm-fringed beach makes way for a stylish reception area. The ethos of this image-conscious office is clear. "Aunty Beryl" is a young, attractive icon for a youthful, dynamic firm of architects, purveyors of seductive images. For a firm of architects, the receptionist sets the tone for a celebration of the image that governs the whole ethos of the office. It is the image that is celebrated here, a calculated stage set in which glossy brochure, vase of flowers, and smiling, pretty receptionist all play their part.[36] The glamorous world of the designer office is treated at the same level as the exotic world of a desert island paradise.

What are we to make of these parallels? The Bacardi commercial, on the one hand, plays upon a contrast between the real world and a dream world. The message is clear enough: the narcotic effect of Bacardi will provide a form of ecstatic escapism from the tedium of everyday life. The architects' recruitment advertisement, on the other hand, plays upon a different contrast. The humdrum image of "The Dog 'n' Duck down the High Street," for example, is contrasted not with an exotic beachside bar from a dreamworld, but with the chic high-tech interior of an eminently real designer bar. There is a secondary mechanism at work. The highly aestheticized world of a designer interior, by implication, is not only comparable to the intoxicating world of Bacardi but also produces a precisely similar effect. The advert highlights the anaesthetizing effect of the aesthetic. Just as the bombardment of sensory stimulation sets up a defensive mechanism in the individual, as Benjamin had observed, causing consciousness to act as a form of buffer to the external world and engendering a desensitized, blasé outlook, so too the heightened aesthetic environment of the world of design creates its own sensory cocoon.

What is at work here is aestheticization in its most potent form. An implicit parallel is drawn between the effects of Bacardi and the intoxicating effects of working in the aesthetic environment of an architectural office. It is as though the anaesthetizing effect of the aesthetic moment—the numbing that Benjamin had observed—replicates the narcotic effect of alcohol. Just as Bacardi is purported to transport the drinker into an imaginary realm displaced from the grim reality of "Peckham on a Monday night," so the second advert, while remaining within the space of the High Street, seeks to transport the viewer into an aestheticized version of the real. The aesthetic environment of an architectural office will provide you with an ecstatic experience comparable to drinking alcohol. Aestheticization has a similar effect to Bacardi.

4

THE ARCHITECTURE OF THE CATWALK

If aestheticization induces a form of *anaesthesis,* the effects will be particularly pronounced in a culture that has already become heavily aestheticized. A society awash with images will experience a consequent reduction in social and political sensibilities, as the intoxication of the image leads to a lowering of critical awareness. The saturation of the image will therefore promote an uncritical acceptance of the image. Saturation, intoxication, complacency. And this process will loop back on itself as complacency permits further saturation. The intoxication of the aesthetic creates an aesthetics of intoxication. Blue Lagoon, Tequila Sunrise, Black Lady. It is a culture of the cocktail, an addictive obsession with the narcotics of the image, with an ever-decreasing sense of critical awareness. Aestheticization leads to anaesthetization leads to further aestheticization in a dizzying spiral whose only apparent respite lies in the total collapse of the system under its own intoxication. It is this addiction to the image that marks late capitalist society.

The French artist and critic Guy Debord was one of the first to recognize and address this emerging obsession with the image. Debord noted how by the 1960s the image had displaced reality. While Baudrillard was to extend this thesis for our contemporary moment, observing that we have now entered a culture of complete simulation, Debord captured with remarkable lucidity the early developments in this process. His 1967 book *La société du spectacle,* subsequently translated into English as *The Society of the Spectacle,* constitutes a form of theoretical manifesto for the Situationist International, a loose-knit, revolutionary group of artists and intellectuals founded in 1957.[1] In it he offers a telling and prescient critique of late capitalism, where everything is immediately coopted into images and commodities. Long before the media society had fully developed, long before advertising and other blandishments of a consumer culture had taken a firm hold, Debord recognized the symptoms of a society utterly preoccupied with the image. Indeed, so dominant is the role of the image in contemporary life that society itself has become a spectacle.

In *The Society of the Spectacle* Debord comments on how the capitalist framework presents society in terms of superficial, commodified images. "The whole life of those societies in which modern conditions of production prevail presents itself as an immense accumulation of *spectacles*. All that once was directly lived has become mere representation."[2] Debord is clearly indebted here to the work of Karl Marx, who had recognized the alienation of the worker from the means of production, and likewise to Walter Benjamin, who had elaborated a similar thesis in analyzing the cult of the commodity under capitalism. But whereas for Marx and Benjamin this alienation was that of the workers from their goods, for Debord the alienation of today is that of the people from themselves. In the society of the spectacle, reality has been so obscured beneath an accumulation of images—of "spectacles"—that it is no longer possible to experience it directly. Late capitalism had spawned a society of alienated individuals who have lost all sense of any genuine ontological experience.

This condition, as Sadie Plant has observed, has serious consequences:

The situationists . . . argued that the alienation fundamental to class society and capitalist production had permeated all areas of social life, knowledge and culture, with the consequence that people are removed and alienated not only from the goods they produce and consume, but also from their own experiences, emotions, creativity, and desires. People are spectators of their own lives, and even the most personal gestures are experienced at one remove.[3]

It is precisely in the context of a society of affluence, a society awash with consumer products, that this condition has developed. For it is the very essence of contemporary marketing to convince the consumer that a product is not only useful but necessary. This myth of consumption fuels the alienation in the society of the spectacle: "If modern society is a spectacle, modern individuals are spectators: observers seduced by the glamorous representations of their own lives, bound up in the mediations of images, signs, and commodities."[4]

In this world of the Kodak camera, of *Paris-Match* magazine, people can only perceive themselves as though they are being captured on celluloid or featured on the glossy pages of glamorous magazines. It is a world of appearances propagated by the media, a commodified world of advertising which sells you an image of yourself. "You, too, could look like this." It is a world of beauty parlors, fashion catwalks, dyed hair and false eyelashes, a cosmetic world that re-presents reality and dictates taste. It is a world, above all, of the advertising billboard. For the billboard captures most articulately the power of the commodified image. The billboard sells not just a product but a lifestyle. This situation threatens to render the individual powerless as the marketplace comes to dictate what might be permissible. Furthermore, such "experiences" as there are can only be in essence secondhand. One has to conform and subscribe to a predetermined model; the possibility of any active participation in the construction of the lived world has been all but erased.

But the outlook of the Situationists was not totally pessimistic, for they recognized the internal resistance in the society of the spectacle. As Sadie Plant comments, "The subjectivity which produces, consumes, and is itself produced and consumed by the Spectacle is already busy looting it as well. It does not passively consume and obediently produce, as the Spectacle ostensibly intends: it sabotages, steals, plays in the supermarkets, and sleeps on the production line."[5] The Situationists devised various strategies informed by this tendency as a means of combating the "spectacle." While their critique was leveled at the aestheticization of the world, their strategies of resistance equally borrowed from that condition. Artistic works, comic strips, and advertisements were plagiarized and subverted through strategies such as *détournement,* which effectively reappropriated them by reversing their perspective. Such strategies were premised on the notion that the most effective way of countering the society of the spectacle was to undermine it from within, using its own internal logic to heighten awareness of the problem. Raoul Vaneigem defined the task as follows: "The spontaneous acts we can see everywhere forming against power and its Spectacle must be warned of all the obstacles in their path and must find a tactic taking into account the strength of the enemy and its means of recuperation. This tactic, which we are going to popularize, is *détournement.*"6

For the Situationists and their related pressure groups, architecture formed a prominent part of the critique of contemporary society. They were highly critical of the abstracted rationality of much modernist architecture, and one of the strands from which the Situationist International had been formed was the International Movement for an Imaginist Bauhaus, which offered an alternative vision for aesthetic expression. A central theme in Situationist thought became that of "unitary urbanism," which viewed the city holistically as a combination of artistic potential and engineering resources. The city, moreover, conditioned everyday life. Whereas many artists and "revolutionaries" failed to engage sufficiently with the built environment, the Situationists saw it as a significant factor in determining the possibilities of lived experience. They recognized that "emotions, desires and experiences" differed "according to the architecture of a space, and the arrangement of colours, sounds, textures and lighting with which it is created."7 They therefore looked to an architecture that fired the imagination and allowed for a richer ontological experience—"moments of life concretely and deliberately lived."8 Ivan Chtcheglov charted a new vision for the city. In his "Formulary for a New Urbanism" he describes a dynamic, responsive architecture that transcends the banal forms of the present. Chtcheglov calls for "rooms more conducive to dreams than any drug, and houses where one cannot help but love." He envisages a city with districts such as a Bizarre Quarter, a Happy Quarter, a Noble and Tragic Quarter, a Sinister Quarter, and so on.[9]

The Situationists attracted a range of sympathetic voices from the world of architecture. Prominent among them was the Dutch architect Constant, whose New Babylon projects, although not fully embraced by the movement, remain the most comprehensive attempt to translate the Situationists' ideals into architectural forms.[10] In these projects Constant pursues themes such as "disorientation" and "dynamic space." Anxious to avoid the limitations of the static spaces of utilitarian society, he promotes the concept of the "dynamic labyrinth," one that accepts that the liberation of behavior requires a labyrinthine space, but one which allows that space to be continually subject to modification, according to the "ludic" imagination. Echoes of these ideas are to found in the subsequent event-architecture of Bernard Tschumi and others.[11]

The city became the key site for their investigations in psycho-geography, investigations aimed at establishing new ways of inhabiting the city. A central concept in this context was the *dérive,* or "drift," a technique of reappropriating the city as an ontological experience. More indebted perhaps to the Surrealists' experiments in automatism—the surrendering of the self to the pleasures of the city—than the Situationists would generally acknowledge, the *dérive* was a practice of exploring the city in which "one or more persons during a certain period drop their usual motives for movement and action, their relations, their work and leisure activities, and let themselves be drawn by the attractions of the terrain and the encounters they find there."[12] Unlike the Surrealists, however, the Situationists did not simply abandon themselves to unconscious desires. While the *dérive* was unplanned—and indeed the Situationists would even employ strategies such as the use of a map from one space to navigate their way through another, as a mechanism of undermining the "plan"—the aim throughout was to *consciously* challenge the hegemony of capitalist property relations in the city. They attempted through the *dérive* to counter the dominant perception of the city as a grid of real estate, and to explore its potential as the site of lived experience.

Central to the outlook of the Situationists was the concept of the "situation," an active spatio-temporal event of lived experience, unshackled from the constraints of the "spectacle." The "situation" was therefore a way to counter the reified existence implicit in the society of the spectacle. In this, the "situation" shared something with the "moment" championed by Henri Lefebvre, a fleeting, intensely euphoric sensation that appeared as a point of rupture revealing the totality of possibilities of daily existence. But whereas Lefebvre's "moment" remained somewhat passive and temporal, the "situation" constituted a form of active, spatio-temporal engagement. And it was the city that formed the site of the ultimate "situation," the uprising of May 1968 in Paris. While one should be wary of ascribing too much influence to the Situationists in this extraordinary series of events, their contribution to raising consciousness and fostering a spirit of resistance—notably through the Situationist-inspired *enragés* movement—should not be underestimated. Demonstrations began with students barricading streets in the Latin Quarter of Paris. The uprising attracted sympathizers and escalated into the throwing of cobblestones and Molotov cocktails and the destruction of police vans. It soon spread to wildcat strikes in factories and workplaces across the country, culminating in a general strike that brought the entire country to a standstill and effectively brought down the Gaullist government. A spontaneous uprising of the population calling for a revolution in everyday life, May '68 proved to be the greatest "situation" of all, revealing the deep unrest at the conditions of contemporary society: "What thus came to the light of consciousness in the spring of 1968 was nothing other than what had been sleeping in the night of 'spectacular society,' whose spectacles showed nothing but an eternal positive façade."[13]

Architecture of the Spectacle

In comparison to the force and polemical nature of the Situationists' work, other aesthetic gestures of that period appear somewhat compromised, trapped within an uncritical domain of capitalistic values.

4.1 Las Vegas. Keith Collie.

Nowhere is this more obvious than in some of the supposedly "radical" theories promoted within architectural circles around that time.

It is perhaps ironic that Debord should publish his book the year after Robert Venturi published *Complexity and Contradiction in Architecture.* While Debord rails against a superficial world of the commodified image, Venturi embraces and actually celebrates it. While Debord sees the world of the commodified image as the source of contemporary alienation in society, Venturi sees it as a source of inspiration for architecture. In *Complexity and Contradiction* Venturi contrasts an image of "Main Street" with one of Thomas Jefferson's buildings in Charlottesville for the University of Virginia. In his book *God's Own Junkyard,* Peter Blake had criticized the chaos of the former and contrasted it to the order of the latter. Venturi challenges this. In terms of its formal composition Main Street is "almost all right."[14] Yet Venturi ignores the issue of content. He seems oblivious to the fact that he is promoting a celebration of consumer society. The billboards he admires were dictated by essentially commercial—and hence consumerist—concerns. Billboards, advertising hoardings, neon signs, and so on—the very emblems of the society of the spectacle that Debord and others had attacked—become for Venturi a model to be followed in architecture.

We might excuse his seemingly uncritical celebration of consumer society as an aberration, an eccentric architectural viewpoint, were it not for the fact that a few years later, writing with Denise Scott Brown and Steven Izenour, he devotes not just one illustration to the commercial street but an entire book. In *Learning from Las Vegas,* these authors celebrate the advertising hoardings of the world's most famous gambling town in the Nevada desert. They are quick to point out, of course, that they are not engaging the commercial activities of Las Vegas. "Las Vegas's values are not questioned here. . . . The morality of commercial advertising, gambling interests and the competitive instinct is not at issue here . . . this is a study of method, not content"—as though dissociating form from content were unproblematic. Although they believe that dealing with social content should be part of an architect's "broader synthetic tasks," they see their own work as an abstract study of form "in isolation," which for them is "a respectable scientific and humanistic activity," so long as all other concerns are "resynthesized in design."[15] Yet it is in their abstract handling of form, and their refusal to engage the context of Las Vegas, that the real problems of the book emerge. In decontextualizing the forms of Las Vegas, they desemanticize them, setting up a pattern that is to haunt them, as we shall see, in their built work. For once one enters an argument of "form for form's sake" where form is abstracted from other

4.2 "Tan Hawaiian with Tanya." Venturi, Scott Brown, and Izenour, *Learning from Las Vegas*, p. 12.

concerns, it is not easy to "resynthesize" these concerns into the form in the final design.

It is this principle of aestheticization, then, that allows Venturi, Scott Brown, and Izenour to remain so oblivious to the socio-political questions at the heart of Las Vegas, to anaesthetize it, and to adopt an approach that is epitomized by their celebration of the advertising hoarding. In *Learning from Las Vegas* they promote an architecture of advertising; the advertising hoarding becomes the ultimate icon that is championed throughout the book. On the front cover they feature a roadside advertisement with a prominent logo, "Tan Hawaiian with Tanya." What then can we read into this image, an image that the authors give such a place of honor? On a straightforward level it supports a culture of the image, a society of the spectacle where individuals are alienated from their true selves and seduced by glamorous representations of their lives. It is a Barbie world of fashion and good looks, a culture of the beauty parlor. Tanya, the ultimate suntanned icon of sixties America, is sold to you by the billboard. "Buy this product, and you, too, could look like Tanya." Yet beyond this, the image reveals the liquidation of meaning in advertising itself. The fetishization of the image generates an uncritical acceptance of the image. It operates within an aestheticized realm where important political and social questions are not addressed. The full significance of Venturi, Scott Brown, and Izenour's celebration of the advertising hoarding begins to emerge. A tanned, bikini-clad figure is used to promote a suntan lotion, in a poster that blatantly exploits female sexuality.

It is perhaps too obvious to remark that advertising exploits women. Capitalism has spawned a society that idolizes the commodity. This culture of the commodity has led to a cult of the commodity, as goods are invested with an aura of sexual allure. But it is not just that commodities have become sexualized. Sex has also become commodified, and nowhere is this more obvious than within the realm of advertising. While men are clearly also involved in advertising, it is women who are particularly at risk. In the culture of late capitalism, dominated as it is by patriarchy, women are more likely to be exploited by the forces of commodification, and it is in advertising that this exploitation is most explicit. Women are treated not as women but as commodified images of women, decorative, sexually charged accoutrements that help sell a product. This is not a celebration of the qualities of women as ontological beings, but a cynical exploitation of them as marketable, commodifiable images. Yet the authors of *Learning from Las Vegas* offer no comment on this important ethical question. By celebrating this display of woman-as-commodified-image, they are effectively sanctioning the exploitation, wallowing in a realm of the uncritical and the superficial. This is all the more ironic given Denise Scott Brown's published criticisms of the patriarchal star system in architecture[16] and the conscious introduction of non–gender specific language in later additions of *Learning from Las Vegas*.[17]

4.3 Brut advertisement with feminist graffiti. Brenda Prince/Format.

Venturi, Scott Brown, and Izenour's celebration of the image finds its architectural expression in their later built works. Here the same principles are to be found. In the Sainsbury Wing, their extension to the National Gallery in London, for example, the steel trusses that straddle the main staircase appear at first sight to be acting as structural members holding up the roof. Closer inspection, however, reveals that they serve merely as applied decoration. These trusses are hung from the ceiling and do not carry even their own weight, let alone that of the roof. They take their rhythm from the mullions of the curtain glass wall that looks out toward the main building of the National Gallery. And this leads the trusses to fall out of line with the window openings on the internal wall opposite, so that on occasions the trusses sit directly over the openings in this wall. This detail only reinforces the ornamental character of the trusses, since the laws of structural engineering dictate that weight-bearing trusses should never be positioned over a window opening.

4.4 Venturi and Rauch, National Gallery extension, London, interior view. Photo: Phil Starling.

Once removed from their original context, once denied the very function that gave them meaning, the trusses have been recoded as nonstructural "decoration." The whole problem of aestheticization is revealed. It is the image that is important here—the image and nothing else. The trusses have become a stylistic device, and their very "recontextualization" as decoration exposes the problems inherent in the abstract handling of form in *Learning from Las Vegas*. For while the authors insist that their abstract study of form "in isolation" is quite acceptable, provided that all other concerns are "resynthesized" in design, it is clear that this is not so easy once the forms themselves have been decontextualized. If context is what gives a form its meaning, to "resynthesize" that form is to give it a different meaning.

On the exterior the same principle applies. The skin of the building is treated as a decorative stone veneer that is literally wrapped around the facade, with little regard for the layout of the interior. The rhythm of the composite pilasters from the main building is compressed, while a row of painted "Egyptian" columns runs along at ground-floor level. The whole building becomes a riot of conflicting

4.5 Venturi and Rauch, National Gallery extension, London, exterior view. Photo: Phil Starling.

styles, as Greek is mixed with Egyptian, the Victorian engineering aesthetic with contemporary curtain walling. The orders, trusses, and other architectural members have been decontextualized and desemanticized. Like Tanya, they have been rinsed of their original meaning and recoded as mere decoration. The spirit of Las Vegas, it would seem, creeps insidiously into Venturi and Scott Brown's built work.

The Aesthetics of Revolution

Learning from Las Vegas is often viewed as a seminal critique of received architectural values. It has been held to question the very fundamentals of architectural composition. The message is straightforward enough. No longer should architects subscribe uncritically to abstract, academic theories of composition. Instead they should learn from Main Street itself.

But how radical is the book's critique? Within architectural culture, to be "radical" is often presented as a political position; the assumption that architecture has an important social and political mission is frequently elided with the question of design. As a consequence, "good design" is often thought to have a significant social and political impact. By extension, what is considered "radical" within the domain of architecture is likewise thought to be "radical" from a sociopolitical perspective. Venturi, Scott Brown, and Izenour even claim that their work is "revolutionary," in that "learning from the existing landscape is a way of being revolutionary for an architect."[18]

It is clear that whereas Le Corbusier used the term "revolutionary"—however misguidedly—in a genuinely social and political sense, Venturi, Scott Brown, and Izenour use it in an aesthetic sense.[19] "Revolution" becomes a political term appropriated by the aesthetic, but one that relies on its original meaning to claim a certain authority. The term has become aestheticized. Such tactics are in evidence throughout the culture of late capitalism. Indeed one of the strengths of capitalism is that it can so successfully redeploy political terms within the realm of the marketplace. Nowhere is this more obvious than in the world of advertising. In one such example, a Russian-looking woman, arm held aloft in "revolutionary" pose, "demands the right" to have a portable phone. In another, an adaptation of Eugène Delacroix's famous painting *Liberty Leading the People* shows a revolutionary dressed in high fashion. "Principles to die for," reads the caption. Liberty, here, has been subverted into some reactionary, libertarian ideal, and "principles" have been stripped of their ethical status and reappropriated in a moralistic defense of sartorial elegance.

We should be wary, therefore, of architectural theorists who claim that their work is "revolutionary." Such claims run merely at the level of the aesthetic, not only appropriating but also aestheticizing the language of the political realm. This problem extends to the "radical" image that many architects like to present. Rather than being "radical" in the true sense, architects are all too often complicit with the workings of the economic and political status quo. Any claims to free agency should therefore be treated with suspicion. There is a danger in confusing a radical aesthetics with a radical politics, and of conflating the aesthetic with the political—a trap, I think, into which architecture frequently falls. Yet it is not that the aesthetic is fundamentally disjoined from the political. A radical aesthetics may in fact mask and even promote a reactionary politics. Architectural culture will always be susceptible to a reactionary politics, not despite its facade of radicalism but precisely because of it, a facade that is no more than a facade of *aesthetic* radicalism.

We might judge the "revolution" of *Learning from Las Vegas* against the backdrop of Raoul Vaneigem's polemical work "The Revolution in Everyday Life." For Vaneigem realizes that "revolution" is fundamentally a question of *praxis*—the product not of aesthetic contemplation but of active participation. While one might perhaps concede that the Situationists were overly optimistic in their hope to change society, they recognized that politics can only be expressed through political action. True "revolution" takes place not in the art gallery but on the streets and in the halls of government. Vaneigem's "revolution" constituted an attempt to overcome the alienation implicit in the commodified relations of the society of the spectacle. Venturi, Scott Brown, and

Izenour's "revolution," by comparison, proves ultimately to be a complacent aesthetic gesture that, far from undermining the dominant culture, serves merely to reinforce it.

The Lessons of Las Vegas

These are the lessons of Las Vegas, the high capital of the society of the spectacle, where sexist billboards greet the visitor and fake centurions stand guard outside a fake "Caesar's Palace." It is a shallow, depthless world where irony rules over content, pastiche over historical sensibility. Nor is it any coincidence, perhaps, that Venturi, Scott Brown, and Izenour should celebrate Las Vegas, city of advertising, city as advertising. Their uncritical treatment of the values of Las Vegas replicates the liquidation of meaning in advertising itself. Las Vegas, city of the desert, whose own desertification of cultural values reflects the degree-zero cultural depth of the desert around it. Las Vegas, city of advertising, whose bewitching enchantment mirrors the attraction of the desert. Las Vegas, the ultimate city not of architecture but of the commodified sign, the empty, seductive triumph of the superficial. It is precisely this celebration of surface, as Baudrillard notes, the radiance of its depthless advertising, that effaces the architecture of Las Vegas and constitutes such an intoxicating form of seduction:

When one sees Las Vegas at dusk rise whole from the desert in the radiance of advertising, and return to the desert when dawn breaks, one sees that advertising is not what brightens or decorates the walls; it is what effaces the walls, effaces the streets, the facades and all the architecture, effaces any support and any depth, and that it is this liquidation, this reabsorption of everything into the surface . . . that plunges us into this stupefied, hyperreal euphoria that we would not exchange for anything else, and that is the empty and inescapable form of seduction.[20]

SEDUCTION, THE LAST RESORT

Las Vegas, for Baudrillard, is trapped within a depthless world of appearances, where everything is "liquidated" and "reabsorbed" into the surface. This is the logic of seduction (in its broadest sense, and not in the narrow sense of *sexual* seduction). Seduction, Baudrillard argues, is that which extracts meaning from discourse and detracts it from its truth.[1] Seduction attempts to enchant the viewer on a purely visual level and to prevent any deeper level of inquiry. Seduction can therefore be contrasted to "interpretation." Whereas interpretation strives to rupture the realm of surface appearances and inquire after some underlying truth, seduction seeks to bewitch the viewer within the enchanting world of the surface, never to look beyond. By dallying within the realm of appearances, seduction stifles any quest for meaning. "All appearances," as Baudrillard notes, "conspire to combat and root out meaning (whether intentional or otherwise), and turn it into a game, into another of the game's rules, a more arbitrary rule—or into another elusive ritual, one that is more adventurous and seductive than the directive line of meaning."[2]

It is not that Baudrillard is opposed to seduction itself. Indeed, he champions "seduction" over the opposite model of "interpretation." And he is especially critical of the domain of psychoanalysis, for so long obsessed with questions of interpretation. Although Freud himself had once worked with the concept of seduction, he later abandoned it, as

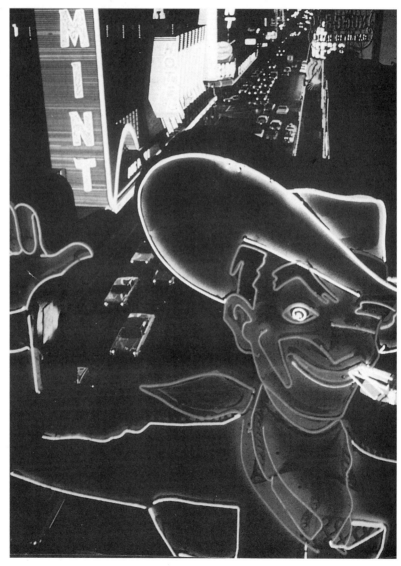

5.1 Las Vegas. John Launois.

Baudrillard notes, for more instrumental models of analysis: "Freud abolished his theory of seduction, in order to put into place a machinery of interpretation, and of sexual repression, that offer all the characteristics of objectivity and coherence."[3] But seduction has come back with a vengeance to haunt psychoanalysis through Lacanian discourse, "in the wild-eyed form of a play of signifiers." This for Baudrillard itself led to the death of psychoanalysis, as "the most beautiful construction of meaning ever erected thus collapses under the weight of its own signs."[4]

Baudrillard therefore champions "seduction" over all forms of "meaningful discourse." For "meaningful discourse" is in its essence unseductive, and herein lies its downfall. Language, with its subtle nuances and plays of meaning, delights in the very attraction of its appearance. Although "meaningful discourse" may collude with "seduction," whenever it tries to counter the very allure of "seduction" it threatens to be seduced from its path by the play and aleatory charm of language. Hence "meaningful discourse" will always lose out to seduction.

But what is important for Baudrillard is that there has been a genealogy of the concept of "seduction." The seduction that Baudrillard champions is one that, perhaps, has already been lost. There was a "golden age" of seduction, when "seduction," "valor," and "honor" were all part of a courtly world. But with the advent of the industrial revolution, seduction became eclipsed by an emphasis on "production," with its concern to make everything clear and objectifiable. Seduction, Baudrillard observes, is derived from the Latin *seducere,* "to take aside," "to divert from one's path," whereas production is derived from *producere*—which can mean "to render visible" or "to make appear."[5] The contemporary world is dominated by "production." "Everything," Baudrillard notes, "is to be produced, everything is to be legible, everything is to become real, visible, accountable; everything is to be transcribed in relations of force, systems of concepts or measurable energy; everything is to be said, accumulated, indexed and recorded . . . a culture of monstration, demonstration, and productive monstrosity."[6] Seduction, with its enigmatic, mysterious play of appearances, its intrigues and subtle ruses, is quite different from all this. Seduction is totally opposed to production. "Seduction removes something from the order of the visible, while production constructs everything in full view, be it an object, a number or concept."[7]

Attitudes to the body reflect deeper cultural conditions. Just as for Simmel the abstracted circulation of capital in a society dominated by exchange value came to be reflected in the abstract circulation of individuals in the modernist metropolis, so too for Baudrillard the mechanization of the lifeworld in a society dominated by technology has been replicated in the dominant functionalistic attitude to the body and the sexual act. "Ours is a culture of premature ejaculation," writes Baudrillard; "our center of gravity has been displaced towards a libidinal economy concerned with only the naturalization of desire, a desire dedicated to drives, or to a machine-like functioning, but above all, to the imaginary of repression and liberation."[8] Once sex is treated as a function, the influence of seduction begins to wane. This is not to associate seduction merely with the domain of the sexual. Of course, the two have come to be related, but this was not always the case. In an age when the symbolic order still held sway, sex was only an "addendum" to seduction. Now all this has been reversed. It is only in our present culture that "the sexual has triumphed over seduction and annexed it as a subaltern form."[9] In all aspects of cultural life production has eclipsed seduction. And it is in the figure of pornography that production manifests itself within the sphere of the sexual—"the obscene scene of the real," where all veils are removed, and where the body becomes monstrously visible. Pornography is an orgy of realism, an orgy of production.

With the shift in emphasis toward production, seduction has lost some of its vital force. It has become dissipated until what we have today is but a straitened, degraded version to match our era of mechanization. Just as the sexual has degenerated into the pornographic, so seduction today has been reduced to a mechanized, depthless strategy. "A fantastic reduction of seduction," as Baudrillard observes. "This sexuality transformed by the revolution of desire, this mode of bodily production and circulation has acquired its present character, has come to be spoken of in terms of 'sexual relations,' only by forgetting all forms of seduction."[10] Seduction has been caught in a discursive libidinal striptease. In this society of exchange, seduction is now everywhere and nowhere, supporting the circulation of exchanges and oiling social relations. And it is precisely the meaninglessness of this circulation that highlights the impotence of our contemporary seduction. We can no longer speak of seduction versus meaning, since, for Baudrillard, the world has lost all its meaning. Nor is there any truth to subvert. Seduction itself has been trapped, rendered impotent, in an endless flotation of signs that have come adrift from any sense of reference. In an age obsessed with production, meaning has given way to technique and performativity. It is no longer a question of "why?" but "how?" and "how often?"

Seduction has lost its charm. It has lost all its passion. "Corrupted of its literal meaning which implies charm and mortal enchantment," this dissipated seduction "comes to signify the social and technical lubrication required for smooth relations—a smooth semiurgy, a soft technology. . . . Soft energy, soft seduction."[11] This "soft" seduction proliferates everywhere in today's society. It is a weakened seduction, synonymous, in Baudrillard's eyes, "with so much else in this society— the ambience, the manipulation, the persuasion, the gratification, the strategies of desire, the mystique of personal relations, the libidinal economy and its smoothed over relations of transference which relays the competitive economy and its relations of force."[12]

In this degeneration of "seduction" there are echoes of the evolution of attitudes to art. Benjamin notes how the work of art had its origin as a ritual object in cults, before becoming secularized as a cultural or aesthetic form, and then finally succumbing to its pure form with the decline of aura in the age of mechanical reproduction, when the work of art loses its unique quality and no longer holds much value. Seduction, too, has its origins in the ritual, before shifting to its aesthetic phase, where seduction becomes a game, a play of surface appearances. The next stage would be one where, like art, seduction would be reduced to "the endless reproduction of a form without content."[13] This stage, one might surmise, has already been reached.

The Seduction of Las Vegas

Here we find ourselves returning to the rhetoric of *Learning from Las Vegas*. For it is precisely the image of Las Vegas as a totally contentless form that Venturi, Scott Brown, and Izenour wish to promote. It is, after all, a study "of method, not content."[14] It is no longer a question of ethics or meaning, but simply "form" in its stripped-down, obscene state: form for form's sake. What counts for them in Las Vegas is not the battle of form versus content, aesthetics versus ethics, or indeed seduction versus meaning. Rather it is the banal encounter between form and form. And yet they argue for "an architecture of persuasion," an architecture, that is, that seems to appeal to seduction. In what sense, then, can Las Vegas be seen as seductive? Is it that soft, pervasive form of seduction that reproduces itself everywhere? Is it that substanceless, senseless form of seduction that marks the eventual triumph and dissolution of seduction? And, certainly, if Baudrillard himself recognizes in Las Vegas a certain version of seduction, one that he describes as "that empty and inescapable form of seduction," we can be sure that the principle that underpins this "architecture of persuasion" is precisely the ultimate degraded version, a version of seduction that reveals the shadowless obscenity of the present.

In this respect the gambling in Las Vegas acts as a mirror to that condition. For if the final stage of seduction takes on a totally mechanized, contentless form, this is itself reflected in the game of gambling, which Benjamin compares to the experience of the worker in the factory. The mechanization of the process of gambling replicates the mechanization of the factory machine, while the "drudgery of the laborer" is in its own way a counterpart to the drudgery of the gambler. "Gambling," Benjamin notes, "even contains the workman's gesture that is produced by the automatic operation, for there can be no game without the quick movement of the hand by which the stake is put

Plate 1 Night sky over Baghdad, Iraq, January 16, 1991. Grazia Neri.

Plate 2   Manhattan. Francisco Hidalgo.

Plate 3   Las Vegas. Keith Collie.

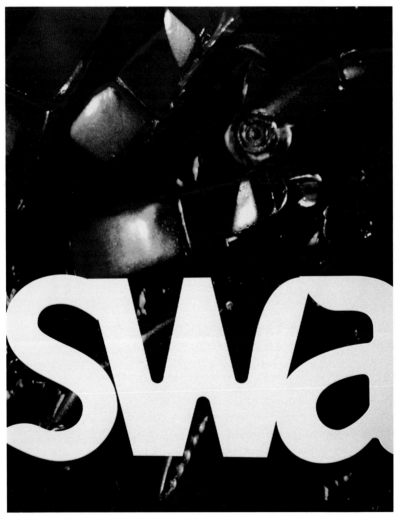

Plate 4 "Swarm." Kevin Rhowbotham, *Form to Programme*, p. 62.

down or a card is picked up. The jolt in the movement of a machine is like the so-called *coup* in a game of chance."[15]

As the workmen come to replicate the abstract motion of the machine with their own actions, so the gamblers take on a distracted air. "They live their life as automatons," as Benjamin observes, "and resemble Bergson's fictitious characters who have completely liquidated their memories."[16] For distraction as a form of leisure-time entertainment becomes the complement of a working day filled with meaningless repetition. Like is replaced with like. Leisure folds into business and takes from it its own essential characteristics, its own shallowness of outlook. Surface-level entertainment comes to compensate for the tedium of surface-level work, as distraction takes on the role of "free-time busy-ness."[17] Distraction becomes a form of business.[18]

If, paradoxically, the repetitive mechanized action of the machine may serve to desensitize the nervous system and anaesthetize the workman, so too the empty repetitive jolts of the one-armed bandits, the flashing lights, the exotic cocktails, and the sensory bombardment of the amusement arcade may provide their own form of aesthetic cocoon. The visual and acoustic kaleidoscope of sensations leaves the gambler blasé, intoxicated, enveloped in a narcotic, trancelike state, such that the gambling world takes on a curious mythic dimension. The abstract machinery of gambling becomes invested with quasi-religious powers, and it is precisely this mythic dimension that hides the shallow banality at its heart. Beneath the glitter and the showering of special effects lurks the crude business ethos of commercial enterprise. It is through the vulgar instrumentality of capitalism that seduction has been contaminated. Seduction has been put at the service of production. The "seduction" of gambling is therefore caught within the obscene pornographic logic of the striptease.

Las Vegas embodies a depthless, contentless form of seduction, a degraded version of the original sense of seduction still evident in Europe. It is a "seduction" somehow without seduction, a shadowless version, a "seduction" of "superficial saturation and fascination." For it is in this final phase, as Baudrillard hints, that seduction may simply lapse into "fascination." In the extreme condition where seduction as empty, meaningless play comes to dominate everything, the notion of play is devalued. In a country such as America, "play" becomes mindless switching among eighty-three different TV channels. "Play" comes to represent not seduction but a banal circulation of systems—"astral" America. It is here, then, that "play" as the endless, combinatory game of mixing and changing comes to be a source of fascination. "One can no longer speak of a sphere of enchantment or seduction," notes Baudrillard; "instead, an era of fascination is beginning."[19] And the fascination of the obscenity of Las Vegas comes to mirror the fascination of the empty intensity of the desert, with its infinite, undifferentiated vistas and its brilliant neutrality. Las Vegas, like the desert, becomes the vanishing point of culture. In this, Las Vegas comes to stand for what Baudrillard sees as the cultural desert of America itself, a land that does not know the true sense of seduction:

No charm, no seduction in all this. Seduction is elsewhere, in Italy, in certain landscapes that have become paintings, as culturalized and refined in their design as the cities and museums that house them. Circumscribed, traced-out, highly seductive spaces where meaning, at these heights of luxury, has finally become adornment. It is exactly the reverse here: there is no seduction, but there is absolute fascination—the fascination of the very disappearance of the aesthetic and critical forms of life in the irradiation of the objectless neutrality.[20]

The Architecture of Seduction

Evidently, then, an architecture that aims at seduction yet claims to offer some sense of radical critique must be compromised. The many projects of the so-called avant-garde that fetishize the image are caught within this paradox. The fetishizing of the image, by subscribing to the logic of seduction, cannot also seek authority in a radical critique of contemporary architectural culture. For radical critique defines itself as a politics of content that operates at the level of meaning. Seduction, meanwhile, operates at a surface level and serves to counter any political critique and any quest for meaning. It is not that politics is ever fully divorced from seduction. Indeed seduction plays a key role in the

5.2 Kevin Rhowbotham, *Form to Programme,* front cover.

process of political solicitation. Where meaningful discourse falters, seduction takes over. In politics seduction acts as a beguiling trap, a surface gloss, to entice and distract the voter. It lures its victim by absorbing and stifling any sense of inquiry. The force of seduction runs contrary to the force of critical inquiry. Although critique may be seductive, seduction can never be critical.

The paradox comes out most clearly in Kevin Rhowbotham's *Form to Programme,* a book noble in its intentions and illustrated with attractive enough images, but flawed in its overall conclusions.[21] Rhowbotham's book is one of the most striking of recent attempts in the avant-garde world of London schools of architecture to establish a new direction in architectural education. As its title suggests, the book aims to invert the traditional modernist dictum of "form follows function," by exploring the possibility of form that "emerges as a consequence of experimentation and refinement."[22] The notion of "programme" is only introduced "after formal experimentation is compositionally resolved, at the end, rather than the beginning of the familiar project cycle." Sensuously illustrated with student work, the book charts a series of strategies—"auto-dynamism," "the scratch," "mapping," "parasites," "appropriations," "territorialities"—by which to formulate a new approach, in which the hegemony of "content" is displaced as form is championed. For Rhowbotham, "form is the primary means of political engagement at the level of cultural critique."[23]

David Greene's introduction to the book is superimposed on an image of a beach, and is titled—somewhat ironically, it would seem—with the Situationist slogan "Beneath the pavement is the beach." Here Greene unwittingly exposes how this project is caught within a double bind. At the heart of this problem lies the question of seduction. On the one hand Greene champions seduction; on the other hand he argues for the need for content, as though the "manifest discourse" of seduction can be reconciled seamlessly with the "latent discourse" of content. He bemoans the current trend in which much student work tends to be "drained of concept," and then goes on to claim that "its means of seduction is through the eye, not the mind." This visual seduction, he notes, is facilitated by the use of the computer, and while the possibilities opened up are positive ones, they necessitate a "shift" in "the emphasis of speculative production . . . to another site."[24] This new site, for Greene, is the conceptual.

The paradox becomes clearer when Greene acknowledges a certain discrepancy between the text and the illustrations. "The text," he notes, "subverts and questions, whereas the way that the student projects are set up prohibits such positions." He tries to defend this by arguing for different roles for the text and the images: "It is preferable to view the images in the book as a means of seducing the reader into the text, rather than illustrations of it. In this way a conceptual position can be maintained and closure or default into another mythical realm avoided. By conceptual position, I mean a realm of ideas operating independently of appearances." The appearance, for Greene, always threatens to "anaesthetize" the student into a "condition of mindless consumption." This is an important point which leads him to posit that images themselves are potentially compromised, and that it is up to the text to salvage some form of content. "Just suppose for a minute," he concludes—very revealingly—"that the text of *Form to Programme* had been submitted without illustration."[25]

Perhaps all this might be explained by the particular type of seduction that Greene celebrates: "At no time in history has the technique available for the production of seductive surface been so rich, varied, extraordinary and accessible. I might therefore argue that seduction has never been easier, or for that matter so prevalent that we no longer recognize the act."[26] We might recognize the "seduction" of which Greene speaks as precisely the "soft" form of seduction identified by Baudrillard, which "permeates the entire expanse of language" and "whose weakened condition has become synonymous with so much else in society."[27] We might recognize, too, that Greene associates the two terms "seduction" and "production"—"the production of seductive images"—that Baudrillard goes to such pains to contrast. This would further corroborate the conclusion that what we have here is a "seduction" from the age of "production," a "seduction," that is, in its most degraded, contemporary form. Seduction becomes a project in the age of mechanization, born of and produced by the technical paraphernalia of that age.

5.3 "Swarm." Rhowbotham, *Form to Programme,* p. 62.

5.4 "Swarm." Rhowbotham, *Form to Programme*, p. 63.

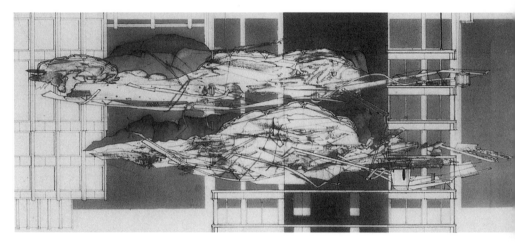

5.5 Parasite
addition to
the Economist
Building,
London.
Rhowbotham,
*Form to
Programme*,
p. 30.

It is a seduction, moreover, inextricably linked to aestheticization. When meaningful discourse has been absorbed and rendered impotent within the depthless, aestheticized world of the image, seduction remains the only viable strategy for winning over the viewer. In a culture of aestheticization, all that is left is seduction. Not only that, but aestheticization prepares the ground for seduction. Just as in everyday life where alcohol may play an important role in seducing a potential customer into buying an artwork, or in persuading a prospective lover to succumb to an amorous advance, so the intoxication of the aesthetic facilitates the possibility of seduction. The image contains within itself the seeds of its own seductive potential.

And yet the really worrying consequence of Greene's observations is not the use of this term, "seduction," in connection with images, but the concern as to whether it might equally be applied to the accompanying text. For in the text itself, one might argue, this soft, pervasive seduction has also left its mark. And indeed Greene seemingly calls for a seduction not only of the retinal but also of the conceptual. One might infer from his championing of the conceptual and his criticism of student work whose "means of seduction is through the eye" that he would prefer work that would "seduce through the mind." The concept-laden text, it could be argued, has itself succumbed to the force of seduction.

Rhowbotham's own comments would seem to support this. A key notion for him is that of "surface"; he is concerned not with the meaning of forms but with their "descriptions"—how they appear on the surface. For Rhowbotham, surface is concerned "not with what lies behind the objects which forms represent, but with what lies in front of them, with those qualities which shimmer and sparkle on the surface of form, and which attract rather than denote signification." In his very celebration of surface, Rhowbotham argues for a politics of persuasion and seduction: "Surface, by wilfully embracing the relativity of commodity production, and by concentrating upon the formal terms of persuasion and seduction, re-engages a real politics of communication."[28] In this surface world of persuasion and seduction, what sort of

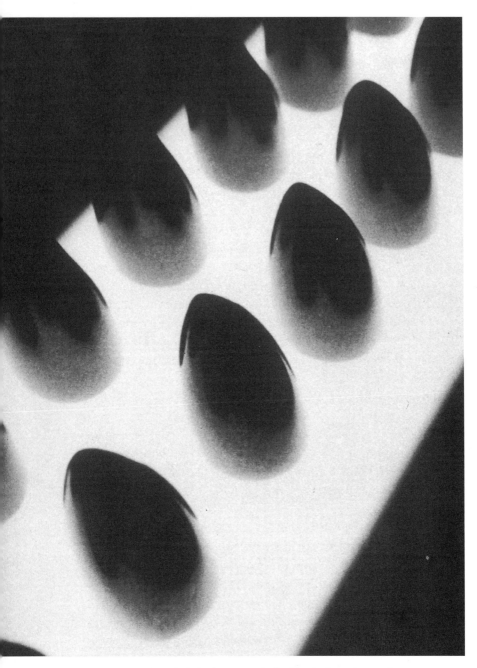

5.6 Exhibition detail, Hochschule der Künste, Berlin. Rhowbotham, *Form to Programme,* p. 42.

politics might we expect to encounter, if not a politics of appearance, a shallow contentless form of politics?

This becomes all the more disturbing when we consider that, for Rhowbotham, surface is what "attracts" signification. Surface is "replete with sticky sites, with hooks that can catch the objects of desire."[29] Are we to assume, then, that this "politics of communication" is merely some floating "object of desire" that is fastened onto the surface? Aside from the obvious relativism that such an approach would suggest, in that potentially *any* "politics" might be fastened to *any* surface, it would also imply that political content might be some free-floating attribute, susceptible to the whole logic of fetishization.

If, furthermore, we are to assume that Greene's "concept" falls into this category, as something that might be attached or added to form, we begin to realize that "concept" or "theory" may themselves be fetishized. Far from being a mechanism to resist fetishization, theory becomes a victim of that process. "The operations of the fetish," as Mark Wigley has observed, "are internalized in the structure of the very theory that identifies and critiques them."[30]

The problem here is that within the depthlessness of our current culture of the instantaneous, the significance of context is eroded. It is this very lack of any sense of context—of historical or geographic specificity—that facilitates the process of fetishization. And certainly it is this that allows the authors of *Learning from Las Vegas* to abstract the forms of Las Vegas and overlook their social significance, and it is this that allows them to reinscribe other such forms in their own built work with so little regard for their original meaning. If we accept that content is not a property of form but merely holds some allegorical relationship with it, the waning of any sense of context or relief within contemporary culture will come to erode that allegorical binding. As such, "theory," "concept," and other terms that represent the "content" of architecture will themselves be detached from the original context that gave them their meaning to become floating "objects of desire" to affix themselves to the "sticky sites" of surface. Theory itself may become a stick-on "object of desire." From this perspective there is perhaps no great rift between the concept-laden text and the sensuous images in the book *Form to Programme*. Both may prove seductive, and both potentially "anaesthetize" the reader into a condition of mindless consumption.

This is a condition, one could argue, that extends to all forms of discourse, critical or otherwise. So virulent has been the aestheticization of the world that the only strategy left is one of seduction, the empty, beguiling play of appearances, where critique loses its force and complacency and fascination take over. Nor does philosophy escape this condition. Indeed we might turn to Debord's own comments on the way that philosophy engages the society of the spectacle. For Debord, the spectacle plays upon all the "weaknesses" in Western philosophy. To this extent, the privileging of sight as the primary mode of perception, and the dominance of a Cartesian rationality that has grown out of this condition, fuel the spectacle itself. Hence philosophy is appropriated as a fundamental aspect of the spectacle. It becomes the medium through which the spectacle operates: "The Spectacle does not realize philosophy," as Debord observes, "it philosophizes reality. The concrete life of everyone has been degraded into a speculative universe."[31]

The elision between an intellectualized existence and a life of heightened exposure to visual stimuli, which Simmel had recognized, underpins this condition. The distracted engagement with the world on the part of the blasé individual replicates the distance opened up by an abstract theoretical outlook. And if the two modes of engagement are so coextensive, is it any wonder that philosophy, the very model of an intellectualized existence, might surrender to the influence of aestheticization? In this context, even philosophers who critique the system are inevitably caught up within that same system. Could it be, then, that Baudrillard himself is the unwitting victim of his own prognosis, and that in the hyperreal world of the image, philosophy itself has become aestheticized, as the ultimate icon of hyperreal culture? More especially, within an architectural culture of depthless, seductive images and shimmering effects, philosophy always threatens to be appropriated as an intellectual veneer, a surface gloss. In such a context, what is philosophy but a mere fashion accessory?

NOTES

1 Saturation of the Image

1. Jean Baudrillard, *The Ecstasy of Communication* (New York: Semiotext(e), 1988).

2. See Jean Baudrillard, "Xerox and Infinity," in *The Transparency of Evil,* trans. James Benedict (London: Verso, 1993), pp. 51–59.

3. Jean Baudrillard, "The Implosion of Meaning in the Media," in *Simulacra and Simulation,* trans. Sheila Faria Glaser (Ann Arbor: University of Michigan Press, 1994), p. 79.

4. Ibid.

5. Ibid.

6. Ibid., pp. 80–81.

7. Jean Baudrillard, *Selected Writings,* ed. Mark Poster, trans. Jacques Morrain (Stanford: Stanford University Press, 1988), p. 190.

8. See Jean Baudrillard, *The Perfect Crime,* trans. Chris Turner (London: Verso, 1996).

9. See Mike Gane, *Baudrillard's Bestiary* (London: Routledge, 1991), p. 101.

10 . As Mike Gane argues, "This displacement has serious consequences. The crucial one is a general aestheticisation of life, as everything falls under the sign of art which nevertheless, and paradoxically, loses all content." Ibid., p. 103.

11. Jean Baudrillard, "Towards the Vanishing Point of Art," quoted in Peter Bürger, "Aporias of Modern Aesthetics," trans. Ben Morgan, *New Left Review* 184 (November/December 1990), 48.

12. Jean Baudrillard, "Transpolitics, Transsexuality, Transaesthetics," trans. Michael Valentin, in William Stearns and William Chaloupka, eds., *Jean Baudrillard: The Disappearance of Art and Politics* (London: Macmillan, 1992), p. 10.

13. Jean Baudrillard, "The End of the Millennium or the Countdown," talk at the Institute of Contemporary Arts, London, June 1997.

14. Baudrillard, "Transpolitics, Transsexuality, Transaesthetics," p. 10.

15. Ibid., p. 14

16. Ibid., p. 12.

17. Ibid., p. 13.

18. Walter Benjamin, *Illuminations,* trans. Harry Zohn (London: Fontana, 1992), p. 235.

19. Fredric Jameson, "Is Space Political?," in Neil Leach, ed., *Rethinking Architecture* (London: Routledge, 1997), p. 258.

20. Fredric Jameson, "The Constraints of Postmodernism" in Leach, ed., *Rethinking Architecture,* p. 254.

21. Yet this is not the allegorical system that one might identify, for example, with Renaissance painting, where allegory relies on a narrative of fixed symbols with which the painter works. The allegory to which I refer is an allegory of association. A closer comparison, therefore, might be the way in which abstract expressionism has been read as political, and even as promoted by the CIA—so the story goes—as a tool of postwar propaganda.

22. "I have come to think that no work of art or culture can set out to be political once and for all, no matter how ostentatiously it labels itself as such, for there can never be any guarantee that it will be used the way it demands. A great political art (Brecht) can be taken as a pure and apolitical art; art that seems to want to be merely aesthetic and decorative can be rewritten as political with energetic interpretation. The political rewriting or appropriation, then, the political use, must be allegorical; you have to know that this is what it is supposed to be or mean—in itself it is inert." Jameson, "Is Space Political?," pp. 258–259.

23. For a model of the way in which content might be understood as a form of "projection," we might consider the work of the artist Krzysztof Wodiczko, who projects politically loaded images onto monuments. (He once projected a

swastika onto South Africa House in London.) While Wodiczko's work aims rather more specifically at a critical reappropriation of monuments as a means of reawakening interest in them, his projection of "content-laden" images onto monuments and buildings echoes the process by which human beings "project" their own readings onto them. On the work of Wodiczko, see, for example, *October* 38 (Winter 1986), "Public Projections" and "A Conversation with Krzysztof Wodiczko," pp. 3–52.

24. Henri Lefebvre, "The Space of Architects," in Leach, ed., *Rethinking Architecture,* p. 144.

25. Theodor Adorno, "Functionalism Today," in Leach, ed., *Rethinking Architecture,* p. 10.

26. Alison and Peter Smithson, *Without Rhetoric: An Architectural Aesthetic 1955–1972* (London: Latimer, 1973), p. 6. Italics added.

27. Ibid., p. 34.

28. Denys Lasdun, *Architecture in an Age of Scepticism* (London: Heinemann, 1984), pp. 137–142

2 The Architect as Fascist

1. On this see Andrew Bowie, *Aesthetics and Subjectivity from Kant to Nietzsche* (Manchester: Manchester University Press, 1990), p. 30.

2. Ansgar Hillach, "The Aesthetics of Politics: Walter Benjamin's 'Theories of German Fascism,'" *New German Critique* 17 (Spring 1979), p. 112.

3. Walter Benjamin, "Theories of German Fascism: On the Collection of Essays, *War and Warrior* edited by Ernst Jünger," trans. Jerolf Wickoff, *New German Critique* 17 (Spring 1979), p. 122.

4. Walter Benjamin, "The Work of Art in the Age of Mechanical Reproduction," in *Illuminations,* trans. Harry Zohn (London: Fontana, 1992), pp. 211–244.

5. Walter Benjamin, *Gesammelte Schriften,* 3:488, quoted in Andrew Hewitt, *Fascist Modernism: Aesthetics, Politics and the Avant-Garde* (Stanford: Stanford University Press, 1993), p. 76.

6. For further discussion of the aestheticization of politics, see Hewitt, *Fascist Modernism.*

7. Albert Speer, quoted in Gitta Seremy, *Albert Speer: His Battle with the Truth* (New York: Knopf, 1995), p. 131.

8. Benjamin, *Gesammelte Briefe,* vol. 2, to G. Salomon Delatour, 10 June 1924, quoted in Momme Brodersen, *Walter Benjamin: A Biography,* trans. Malcolm R. Green and Ingrida Ligers (London: Verso, 1996), p. 139.

9. Filippo Tommaso Marinetti, quoted in Benjamin, "The Work of Art in the Age of Mechanical Reproduction," pp. 234–235.

10. Benjamin, "The Work of Art in the Age of Mechanical Reproduction," p. 234.

11. Ibid., p. 235.

12. Bernard Tschumi, "Six Concepts in Contemporary Architecture," in Andreas Papadakis, ed., *Theory and Experimentation* (London: Academy Editions, 1993), p. 15.

13. In the hyperreal world of simulation, an event does not become an event until it is a media event. From this perspective, the Gulf War did "happen," unlike the massacre of East Timorese by Indonesian forces, about which Western television remained conspicuously quiet. But the way in which the Gulf War "happened" remained locked into a logic of simulation, a world of hyperreality. See Jean Baudrillard, *The Gulf War Did Not Take Place,* trans. Paul Patton (Sydney: Power Publications, 1995).

14. Benjamin, "Theories of German Fascism," p. 128.

15. Lebbeus Woods, *War and Architecture* (Princeton: Princeton Architectural Press, 1993), p. 1.

16. Ibid., p. 24.

17. Ibid., p. 31.

18. Ibid., p. 1.

19. Ibid., p. 19.

20. Ibid., p. 21.

21. Michel Foucault, "Panopticism," in Neil Leach, ed., *Rethinking Architecture* (London: Routledge, 1997), pp. 356–367.

22. Michel Foucault, "Space, Knowledge, Power," in Leach, ed., *Rethinking Architecture,* p. 372.

23. Ibid.

3 The Aesthetics of Intoxication

1. Georg Simmel, "The Metropolis and Mental Life," in Neil Leach, ed., *Rethinking Architecture* (London: Routledge, 1997), p. 70.

2. Ibid., p. 73.

3. Ibid.

4. Ibid.

5. Walter Benjamin, *Charles Baudelaire: A Lyric Poet in the Era of High Capitalism,* trans. Harry Zohn (London: NLB, 1973), p. 56.

6. Graeme Gilloch, *Myth and Metropolis* (Cambridge: Polity Press, 1995), p. 121.

7. Louis Aragon, *Paris Peasant,* trans. Simon Watson Taylor (London: Pan Books, 1987), pp. 77–78.

8. Ibid., p. 130.

9. Ibid., p. 132.

10. Benjamin, *Charles Baudelaire,* p. 132, citing Charles Baudelaire, *Oeuvres,* ed. Yves-Gérard Le Dantec, 2 vols. (Paris: Gallimard, 1954), 2:333.

11. See Margaret Cohen, *Profane Illumination: Walter Benjamin and the Paris of Surrealist Revolution* (Berkeley and Los Angeles: University of California Press, 1993).

12. Gilloch, *Myth and Metropolis,* p. 14.

13. Walter Benjamin, *Illuminations,* trans. Harry Zohn (London: Fontana, 1992), p. 256.

14. Benjamin, *Gesammelte Schriften,* 2:1, 297, quoted in Cohen, *Profane Illumination,* pp. 187–188.

15. Walter Benjamin, *Reflections,* trans. Edmund Jephcott (New York: Schocken, 1986), p. 189.

16. Ibid., p. 55.

17. Benjamin, *Reflections,* p. 137.

18. Ibid., p. 138.

19. Ibid., p. 139.

20. Ibid., p. 179.

21. The following discussion is greatly indebted to the acute observations of Susan Buck-Morss in her now seminal article, "Aesthetics and Anaesthetics:

Walter Benjamin's Artwork Essay Reconsidered," *October* 62 (Fall 1992), pp. 3–41. For a further discussion of this subject see Odu Marquard, *Aesthetica und Anaesthetica* (Paderborn: Ferdinand Schöningh, 1989).

22. Freud's late theory is centered around the conflict between Eros and Thanatos, between "love" and "death," between "life instincts" and "death instincts." Eros, as the "life instinct," serves to counter the tendency toward Thanatos, the "death instinct," and acts as a force to complicate life. Thanatos, that which seeks resolution and quiet, becomes for Freud one of the fundamental impulses within human behavior. The "death instinct" in Freud can be seen to emanate from the moment of birth itself. Birth is seen as a violent trauma that upsets the pleasure of the time in the womb. Yet the memory of this period in the womb remains, and subsequent life is governed by a regressive desire to regain this lost quietude, this lost paradise. The drive toward equilibrium that results is none other than a "continuous descent toward death," which finally provides that longed-for resolution and quiet.

23. Benjamin, *Illuminations,* p. 167.

24. Siegfried Kracauer, *The Mass Ornament,* trans. Thomas Levin (Cambridge: Harvard University Press, 1995), pp. 78–79.

25. Benjamin, *Charles Baudelaire,* p. 134.

26. Freud, *Beyond the Pleasure Principle,* quoted in Benjamin, *Charles Baudelaire,* p. 114.

27. Benjamin, *Charles Baudelaire,* p. 115.

28. Ibid., p. 116.

29. Ibid., p. 117.

30. Ibid., p. 120.

31. Kracauer, *The Mass Ornament,* p. 43.

32. Buck-Morss, "Aesthetics and Anaesthetics," p. 22.

33. Ibid., pp. 22–23.

34. On this see Buck-Morss; also Wlad Godzich, foreword to Paul de Man, *The Resistance to Theory* (Minneapolis: University of Minnesota Press, 1986), p. xiv.

35. Mark Wigley argues precisely the opposite: "The possibility of political critique therefore lies on, rather than behind, the surface. Indeed it requires a certain fetishization of the surface." Mark Wigley, "Theoretical Slippage," in Sarah Whiting, Edward Mitchell, and Greg Lynn, eds., *Fetish* (Princeton: Princeton Architectural Press, 1992), p. 122.

36. The receptionist is exploited here for her image, but this is no innocent image. It is one that has been commodified according to the laws of a strictly gendered marketplace. The attractive, female receptionist has become an object of consumption, so that in effect the receptionist *sells* her sexuality, no less than television hostesses or women used in car advertisements. On this see G. Dyer, *Advertising as Communication* (London and New York: Methuen, 1982), pp. 120–123. This mechanism reaches its extreme manifestation in the case of female models being used to flank the presentation of prizes in male snooker tournaments. On this see J. Hearn and W. Parkin, *"Sex" at "Work": The Power and Paradox of Organisation Sexuality* (Brighton: Wheatsheaf, 1987), p. 102

4 The Architecture of the Catwalk

1. Guy Debord, *La société du spectacle* (Paris: Buchet-Chastel, 1967, and Paris: Editions Champ Libre, 1971). English translations: *The Society of the Spectacle* (Detroit: Black and Red, 1977), and trans. Donald Nicholson-Smith (New York: Zone Books, 1994). It would be wrong to present the Situationists as a coherent group. Along with other related groups, they comprised a loose affiliation of individuals who did not subscribe to any single, unitary outlook. The group was in constant flux, and Guy Debord did not necessarily represent the views of all members. Indeed by 1961 Debord had succeeded in expelling almost all of the original seventy-odd members.
2. Debord, *Society of the Spectacle,* trans. Donald Nicholson-Smith (New York: Zone Books, 1994), p. 12.
3. Sadie Plant, *That Most Radical Gesture* (London: Routledge, 1993), p. 1.
4. Ibid., p. 38.
5. Ibid., p. 86.
6. Vaneigem, "Basic Banalities," reprinted in Ken Knabb, ed. and trans., *Situationist International Anthology* (Berkeley: Bureau of Public Secrets, 1981), p. 125, quoted in Plant, *That Most Radical Gesture,* p. 86.
7. Plant, *That Most Radical Gesture,* 57.
8. Libero Andreotti and Xavier Costa, eds., *Situationists: Art, Politics, Urbanism* (Barcelona: Actar, 1996), p. 14.

9. Ivan Chtcheglov, "Formulary for a New Urbanism," reprinted in Knabb, ed., *Situationist International Anthology,* pp. 3, 4.

10. On this see Andreotti and Costa, eds., *Situationists.*

11. Jacques Derrida has compared the red follies of Tschumi's Parc de La Villette project to dice. In the mutation of their form and the varied activities they invite, the follies play with the "meaning of meaning." See Jacques Derrida, "Point de Folie—maintenant l'architecture," in Neil Leach, ed., *Rethinking Architecture* (London: Routledge, 1997), pp. 324–335.

12. Debord, "Theory of the *Dérive,*" *Internationale Situationiste* 2 (December 1958), reprinted in Knabb, ed., *Situationist International Anthology,* p. 2.

13. Ken Knabb, "The Beginning of an Era," in Knabb, ed., *Situationist International Anthology,* p. 227.

14. Robert Venturi, *Complexity and Contradiction in Architecture* (New York: Museum of Modern Art, 1966), p. 104.

15. Robert Venturi, Denise Scott Brown, and Steven Izenour, *Learning from Las Vegas* (1972; Cambridge: MIT Press, 1988), p. 6.

16. Denise Scott Brown, "Room at the Top? Sexism and the Star System in Architecture," in Ellen Perry Berkeley, ed., *Architecture: A Place for Women* (Washington and London: Smithsonian Institution Press, 1989), pp. 237–246.

17. In the revised edition, as Denise Scott Brown points out, the text has been "de-sexed" and the architect is no longer referred to as "he." Ibid., p. xv.

18. Venturi, Scott Brown, and Izenour, *Learning from Las Vegas,* p. 3.

19. Le Corbusier, of course, actually contrasted his work with revolution. *"Architecture ou Révolution,"* wrote Le Corbusier in 1922. "It is the question of building which lies at the root of the social unrest of today; architecture or revolution." (Le Corbusier, *Towards a New Architecture,* trans. Frederick Etchells [London: Butterworth Architecture, 1989], p. 269. *"Architecture ou Révolution"* was to have been the original title of *Vers une architecture.*) It could be argued, however, that Le Corbusier spoke of avoiding political "revolution" not because he was opposed to the concept of revolution as such, but rather because he recognized in architecture the possibility of a "revolution" that would go beyond the political. As Fredric Jameson has observed, "he saw the construction and the constitution of new spaces as the most revolutionary act,

and one that could "replace" the narrowly political revolution of the mere seizure of power." (Fredric Jameson, "Architecture and the Critique of Ideology," in Joan Ockman, ed., *Architecture, Criticism, Ideology* [Princeton: Princeton Architectural Press, 1985], p. 71.)

20. Jean Baudrillard, "Absolute Advertising, Ground-Zero Advertising," in *Simulacra and Simulation,* trans. Sheila Faria Glaser (Ann Arbor: University of Michigan Press, 1994), pp. 91–92.

5 Seduction, the Last Resort

1. Jean Baudrillard, "On Seduction," in *Selected Writings,* ed. Mark Poster (Stanford: Stanford University Press, 1988), p. 149.

2. Jean Baudrillard, *Seduction,* trans. Brian Singer (New York: St. Martin's Press, 1990), p. 54.

3. Ibid., p. 57.

4. Ibid., p. 58.

5. Ibid., pp. 22, 34.

6. Ibid., pp. 34–35.

7. Ibid., p. 34.

8. Ibid., p. 38.

9. Ibid., p. 41.

10. Ibid., p. 39.

11. Ibid., p. 174.

12. Ibid., p. 178.

13. Ibid., p. 180.

14. Robert Venturi, Denise Scott Brown, and Steven Izenour, *Learning from Las Vegas* (1972; Cambridge: MIT Press, 1988), p. 6.

15. Walter Benjamin, *Charles Baudelaire: A Lyric Poet in the Era of High Capitalism,* trans. Harry Zohn (London: NLB, 1973), p. 134.

16. Ibid., p. 135.

17. Siegfried Kracauer, *The Mass Ornament,* trans. Thomas Levin (Cambridge: Harvard University Press, 1995), p. 325.

18. Baudrillard, *Seduction,* p. 111.

19. Ibid., p. 158.

20. Jean Baudrillard, *America,* trans. Chris Turner (London: Verso, 1988), p. 124.

21. Kevin Rhowbotham, *Form to Programme* (London: Black Dog Publishing, 1995).

22. Ibid., p. 13.

23. Ibid., p. 4.

24. David Greene, "Beneath the Pavement Is the Beach," in Rhowbotham, *Form to Programme,* p. 7.

25. Ibid.

26. Ibid., p. 6.

27. Baudrillard, *Seduction,* p. 178.

28. Rhowbotham, *Form to Programme,* p. 43.

29. Ibid.

30. Mark Wigley, "Theoretical Slippage," in Sarah Whiting, Edward Mitchell, and Greg Lynn, eds., *Fetish* (Princeton: Princeton Architectural Press, 1992), p. 92.

31. Guy Debord, *The Society of the Spectacle* (Detroit: Black and Red, 1983), p. 20, quoted in Andrew Hewitt, *Fascist Modernism: Aesthetics, Politics, and the Avant-Garde* (Stanford: Stanford University Press, 1993), p. 183.

INDEX

Adorno, Theodor W., 11

Advertising, 45–54, 57, 62–65, 69, 70

Aestheticization, 5–15, 32, 88. *See also* Anaesthetics; Architecture, aestheticization of; Image, aestheticizing of; Intoxication, aesthetics of; Politics, and aesthetics; War, aestheticizing of

Affluence, 57

Alienation, 56, 62

Allegory, 8–9, 90nn21,22

Anaesthetics, 44–45, 49

of architecture, 27

Aragon, Louis, 36–37

Architecture

and advertising, 49–54

aestheticization of, 9–15, 27, 32

culture of, 10, 26–27, 49–54, 69

and fascism, 26–27

and liberalism, 31–32

and radical critique, 68–70, 78–80

and seduction, 78–87

Art for art's sake, 17, 18

Art market, 6–7

Aura, 75

Authenticity, 3, 5

Bacardi rum, 46–49, 53–54

Baudelaire, Charles, 35–36, 37, 42, 43

Baudrillard, Jean, vii, viii, 1–3, 5–7, 17, 23, 55, 70, 71–75, 76, 77–78, 81, 88

Benjamin, Walter, vii, 7, 18–22, 26, 27, 32, 35–36, 37–45, 53, 54, 56, 75, 76–77

Bennett, T P, Associates, 49–54

Bentham, Jeremy, 32

Bergson, Henri, 77

Blake, Peter, 62

Blasé outlook, 34–35, 37, 39–40, 45, 49, 54

Brutalism, 11–15

Buck-Morss, Susan, 43, 44

Capitalism, and society, 55–56, 59, 60, 62–64, 68, 77

Ceausescu, Nicolae, 26

Chtcheglov, Ivan, 58

Cigarettes, 46

City, 49, 58–60. *See also* Metropolis, modern

Constant (Constant Nieuwenhuys), 59

Death instinct, 40–41, 94n22

Debord, Guy, viii, 55–56, 62, 95n1

Decontextualization, 9, 63
Delacroix, Eugène, 69
Dérive, 59
Détournement, 58
Disneyland, 3. *See also* Eurodisney
Drugs, 36, 39–40, 44. *See also*
    Intoxication

Enlightenment, 38
Eurodisney, 4–5
Exxon Corporation, 2

Fascism, 18, 22, 26–32
Flaneur, 39–40
Foucault, Michel, 31–32
Freud, Sigmund, 42, 71, 73, 94n22
Functionalism, 11, 74
Futurism, Italian, 21, 27

Gambling, 62, 76–77
Gane, Mike, 89n10
Gray Advertising, 46–49
Greene, David, 80–81, 85, 87
Gulf War, 23–26, 32

Hillach, Ansgar, 17
Hirst, Damien, 14, 15
Hitler, Adolf, 26
Hyperacceleration, 7
Hyperreality, 3–5, 7, 26. *See also*
    Simulation

Image, viii–viii, 45, 55
    aestheticizing of, 5–7, 81, 85
    commodification of, 56, 62
    fetishizing of, 10, 45, 78
Information, 1–2, 7
Information society, 1
International Movement for an
    Imaginist Bauhaus, 58
Intoxication, viii, 53–54
    aesthetics of, viii, 36–40, 45–54, 55
Izenour, Steven, 62–64, 68–70, 76, 87

Jameson, Fredric, 8, 9, 90n22, 96n19
Jefferson, Thomas, 62
Jünger, Ernst, 18

Kant, Immanuel, 11, 17
Kracauer, Siegfried, 41, 43

Lacan, Jacques, 73
Lang, Fritz, 41
Lasdun, Denys, 13
Las Vegas, 61–64, 68–70, 71, 72,
    76–78, 87
Le Corbusier, 68, 96n19
Lefebvre, Henri, 10, 60
Loos, Adolf, 11

Marinetti, Filippo Tommaso, 21, 22
Marx, Karl, 56
Materials, architectural, 13, 15
Meaning, 7–9
    loss of, 2, 5–6
Mechanization, 41–42
Metropolis, modern, 33–40, 41, 43, 74
Mimesis, 40–41
Mussolini, Benito, 26

Narcotics. *See* Drugs
National Socialism (Nazism), 17–22. *See
    also* Fascism
Nietzsche, Friedrich, 17

Paris-Match, 57
Phantasmagoria, 43–44
Philosophy, 88
Plant, Sadie, 56, 57
Poe, Edgar Allan, 41
Politics, and aesthetics, 7–9, 17–22, 23,
    26, 85, 87
Proust, Marcel, 42

Radicalism, cultural and political,
    68–70, 78–80
Reification, 5

Revolution, 68–70, 96n19
Rhowbotham, Kevin, 79–87

Scott Brown, Denise, 62–70, 76, 87
Seduction, viii, 70, 71–88
  and production, 73–74, 77, 81
Sexuality, commodification of, 64, 74,
    75, 95n36
Shock, 40–43, 49
Sign, invisibility of, 1
Simmel, Georg, 33–34, 36, 37, 39–40,
    49, 74, 88
Simulation, 3, 5, 23, 55, 92n13
Situationism, 56–60, 69, 80
Smithson, Alison and Peter, 13
  Hunstanton Secondary Modern School,
    12, 13
Spatial practices, 10, 32
Spectacle (Debord), 55–60, 70, 88
Speer, Albert, 19–21
Stalin, Joseph, 26
Surrealism, 36–40, 59

Tiller Girls, 41
Tourism, 5
Tschumi, Bernard, 23, 59

Unitary urbanism, 58

Vaneigem, Raoul, 58, 69
Venturi, Robert, 62–70, 76, 87
  Sainsbury Wing, National Gallery,
    65–68

War, aestheticizing of, 21, 23–26,
    27–31, 32
Wigley, Mark, 87, 94n35
Wodiczko, Krzysztof, 90–91n23
Woods, Lebbeus, 27–32